AND ITS BACKGROUND Book

The Church of Jesus Grows

NORMAN J. BULL, M.A., Ph.D.

Illustrated by Grace Golden, A.R.C.A.

HULTON EDUCATIONAL PUBLICATIONS

© NORMAN J. BULL 1970
ISBN 0 7175 0454 9

First published 1970 by Hulton Educational Publications Ltd.,
Raans Road, Amersham/Bucks.
Reprinted 1974
Reprinted 1979
Printed in the German Democratic Republic

Contents

Paul

The Church Reaches Europe

Paul the Apostle

The New Testament gives us a wonderfully vivid picture of the beginnings of the Christian Church. The story is told in the "Acts of the Apostles", a fine history book written by Luke, a scholarly Greek doctor. He tells how the Church spread from Jerusalem, far away in the east, to the heart of the great Roman empire—to Rome itself. It is a story of success and of triumph, and its hero is the missionary Paul. The New Testament also contains lively letters, written by Paul to the churches. Luke's history and Paul's letters bring to life the early years of the Church.

No one could have been better prepared to be a missionary than Paul, the hero of the story. He had been brought up at Tarsus, a proud city of Asia Minor, where East and West met together. Thus he was a Hellenist, a Jew who lived outside Palestine. He was surrounded by Hellenism, the Greek culture, and he spoke Greek, the universal language of the Roman world. But Paul came from a devout Jewish home and he had been brought up as a strict Pharisee. He was a scholar of the sacred Law of his people, and he went to the Jewish "university" at Jerusalem to study under the great rabbi Gamaliel. No one could have known Judaism, the religion of the Jews, better than he. Naturally he learnt Hebrew, the language of his people. He must also have known some Latin, the language of the Romans, and the official language of their

7

empire. Thus, wherever he went Paul could make himself understood—whether among Jews, Greeks or Romans—in any part of the empire.

Paul had also been born a Roman Citizen. This was an honoured privilege which placed a man under the special protection of the emperor, wherever he might be. It was an international passport that anyone ignored at his peril. Travel was easy, in the Roman world, both by land and sea. Wherever Paul went he was protected by his Roman Citizenship, he was able to speak in the universal Greek language, and he could find a colony of his fellow-countrymen in every large city he visited.

One thing more was needed to make him a missionary. On the road to Damascus, hurrying there to persecute Christians, he had a wonderful experience of Jesus which gave him his call and his faith. The strict Jew became a dedicated Christian. Now he was ready to suffer and to die for his faith in Jesus. Nothing mattered to him any more compared with his call to spread the Good News of Jesus, the Saviour of mankind.

To all these advantages we must add Paul's own personal gifts. He had great abilities. He was a born leader of men. He was a brilliant and fiery speaker, powerful in proclaiming his faith and in winning men to it. He was a fine organiser, founding and organising and directing his churches. In body he was weak and unimpressive. But that mattered nothing compared with his gifts of mind and heart and tongue. His faith and his dauntless courage triumphed over bodily weakness. No one could have suffered physically more than Paul as he travelled the world to preach the Gospel of Jesus.

THE LIFE AND LETTERS OF PAUL

Life of Paul	Date A.D.	Letters of Paul
Birth of Paul	c.1	
Ministry of Jesus	27-29	
Stoning of Stephen	31	
Conversion of Paul	32	
Paul in the desert oasis	32-34	
Paul's first visit to Jerusalem	34	
Paul at Tarsus	35-44	
Paul with Barnabas at Antioch	44-45	
Paul's 2nd visit to Jerusalem	46	
First Missionary Journey	46-47	Galatians
Council of Jerusalem – Paul's 3rd visit to Jerusalem	49	
Second Missionary Journey	50-52	1 and 2 Thessalonians
Paul's 4th visit to Jerusalem	52	
Third Missionary Journey	53-56	1 and 2 Corinthians
Paul's 5th visit to Jerusalem	56	Romans
Paul a prisoner at Caesarea	56-58	
Voyage to Rome	58-59	
Paul a prisoner at Rome	59-61	Colossians; Philemon; Ephesians; Philippians
UNCERTAIN		
Paul released	61	
Missionary Journeys- West (Spain) East (Crete, Asia Minor Macedonia, Greece)	61-64	
Paul and Peter martyred at Rome	64	1 and 2 Timothy; Titus

Paul the Apostle of the Gentiles

After his experience on the road to Damascus Paul was baptised into the Church. At once he began to proclaim his new faith, but he met with little success. He went away to an oasis in the desert to think out his new beliefs. On his return to Damascus, his preaching brought him enemies among strict Jews, angered by his preaching of Jesus as the Messiah of God. Paul only escaped imprisonment, and possibly death, by being let down in a fish-basket over the city wall. He made his way to Jerusalem. It was only through the friendship of Barnabas, a Hellenist from Cyprus, that Paul won a welcome from the Christians there, naturally afraid of their former persecutor. But at Jerusalem, too, Paul soon made enemies among strict Jews by his preaching. Again he had to flee. His fellow Christians led him safely to the port of Caesarea, and there Paul took ship back to his home city of Tarsus in Asia Minor.

Paul spent ten years at Tarsus and in the surrounding country of Cilicia. There he would have plenty of opportunities to proclaim his faith among Jews in their synagogues, and among Gentiles in the streets and market-places. It is probable that he devoted himself mainly to Jews. Their opposition to him may well account for some of the appalling list of sufferings which he wrote in one of his letters (2 Corinthians 11. 22-30).

Once again Barnabas befriended Paul. He had been sent to Antioch in Syria, 80 miles from Tarsus, by the church at Jerusalem. A church had been founded in Antioch by Hellenist Jews who had left Jerusalem during the persecution in which Paul himself had taken part. The Jewish Christians at Jerusalem were horrified when

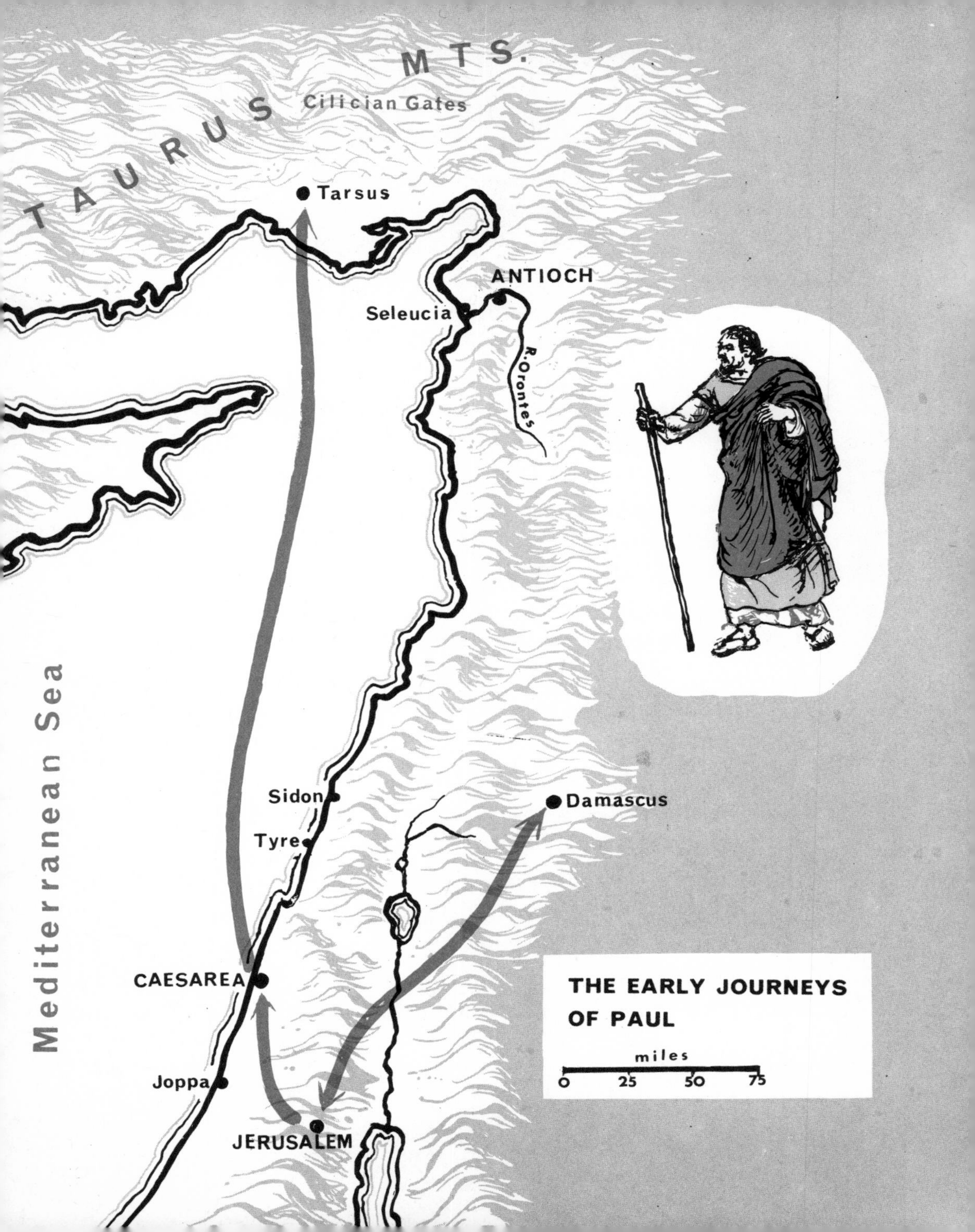

TAURUS MTS.

Cilician Gates

Tarsus

ANTIOCH

Seleucia

R. Orontes

Mediterranean Sea

Sidon

Tyre

Damascus

CAESAREA

Joppa

JERUSALEM

THE EARLY JOURNEYS
OF PAUL

miles

0   25   50   75

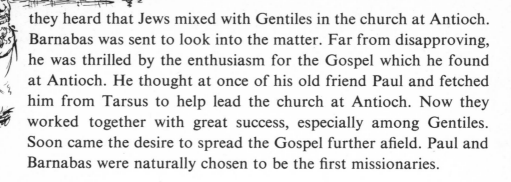

they heard that Jews mixed with Gentiles in the church at Antioch. Barnabas was sent to look into the matter. Far from disapproving, he was thrilled by the enthusiasm for the Gospel which he found at Antioch. He thought at once of his old friend Paul and fetched him from Tarsus to help lead the church at Antioch. Now they worked together with great success, especially among Gentiles. Soon came the desire to spread the Gospel further afield. Paul and Barnabas were naturally chosen to be the first missionaries.

Paul the missionary

Paul's work among Gentiles at Antioch was to set the pattern for his life's work as the "apostle of the Gentiles". He set off, on this first missionary journey, to Cyprus, the home of his companion Barnabas. Then the missionaries sailed to the mainland of Asia Minor. Paul had already spread the Gospel and founded churches in his native Cilicia. Now he travelled inland, further west, establishing churches at Pisidian Antioch, Iconium, Lystra and Derbe. The missionaries went first to the Jewish colony, if there was one, when they came to a town. There they proclaimed the Christian Gospel in the synagogue, where they had a ready-made audience. Jews would form the bulk of the congregation. But there were also God-fearers at the synagogue service. They were high-minded Gentiles who accepted the Jewish faith and morality and tried to live by them. But they never became full Jews because they could not accept customs in the Jewish Law which were strange to them.

The God-fearers welcomed the Christian preaching warmly. It offered all that attracted them to Judaism—belief in one righteous God, Creator and Lord of heaven and earth, and a noble way of

12

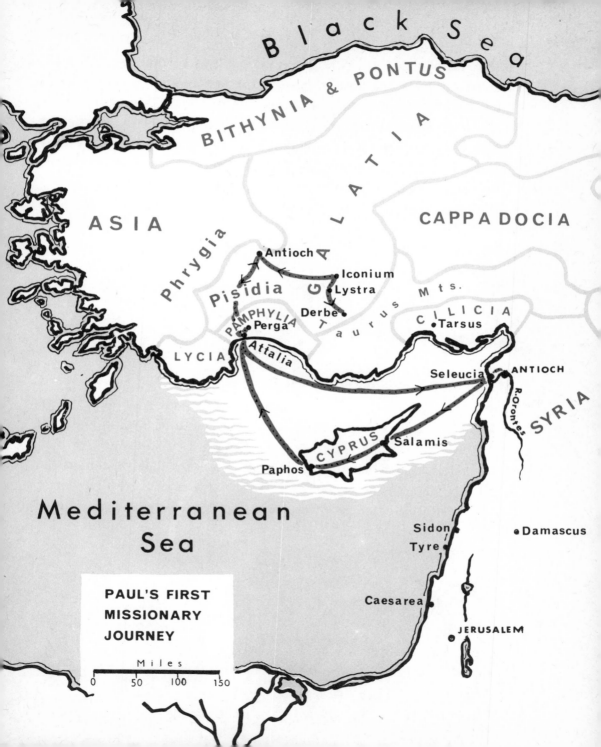

Black Sea

BITHYNIA & PONTUS

G A L A T I A

ASIA

CAPPADOCIA

Phrygia

Pisidia

Antioch

Iconium
Lystra

Derbe

Taurus Mts.

CILICIA

Tarsus

PAMPHYLIA

Perga

Attalia

LYCIA

Seleucia

ANTIOCH

R. Orontes

SYRIA

CYPRUS

Salamis

Paphos

Mediterranean
Sea

Sidon
Tyre

Damascus

Caesarea

JERUSALEM

PAUL'S FIRST
MISSIONARY
JOURNEY

Miles

0   50   100   150

life. It made none of the strange demands of the Jewish Law—circumcision, food laws, sabbath observance, and the lower place given to women. God-fearers flocked into the Church. Jews became jealous of the success of the Christian preachers among the God-fearers. They were angered, too, by the preaching that their great Messiah, the divine deliverer, had come as a peasant carpenter who had been crucified as a felon and was therefore accursed. Paul was persecuted by fanatic Jews and hounded from town to town. But he courageously revisited the churches he had founded before sailing back to Syrian Antioch.

This first missionary journey (A.D. 46-47) had lasted two years, and the missionaries had travelled 1,400 miles by land and sea. The Church had been established on the island of Cyprus and, still further, on the mainland of Asia Minor. Christians at Antioch were delighted when they heard how Gentiles had welcomed the Gospel, and how they had received the power of the Spirit. There could be no greater proof that God welcomed men of all nations into his church.

Jews and Gentiles in the Church

It was hard for the Jewish Christians at Jerusalem to believe this. They had been brought up strictly by their sacred Law to have nothing to do with Gentiles. Some of them came to Antioch. They insisted that Gentiles must accept the Jewish Law, and so become full Jews, if they wished to receive the promises of God in his Church. They would not sit down at table with Gentiles in the meal of fellowship. Thus they broke up the Christian family; they made Gentiles inferior to Jews in the Church. Paul was very angry. He saw clearly what was at stake. Men were saved by faith in Jesus—not by the Law. Baptism was the way of entry into the Church—not circumcision. Jesus had come as the saviour of all men—not of the Jews alone. God welcomed men of all nations into his Church. The proof was that the Spirit of God had come upon Gentiles. This matter had to be settled once and for all.

Paul and Barnabas were sent by the church at Antioch to Jerusalem. There they met with the apostles and the other leaders of the church to discuss the whole question of Jews and Gentiles in the Church. This Council of Jerusalem took place in A.D. 49. It was decided that Gentiles need not be troubled—that is, they need not accept the Jewish Law. But they must give up all their former pagan ways. They must have nothing more to do with heathen sacrifices or feasts or banquets. Thus the leaders of the Church agreed that Jews and Gentiles were equal in the family of God. They could live together in the Church, sharing in worship and in fellowship together.

Official letters were written stating these decisions. They were addressed to the Gentile churches of Asia Minor. They were to be taken to the mother church of the Gentiles at Syrian Antioch by two leading members of the Jerusalem church. One was Judas Barsabas, a Jew of Judaea. The other was Silas, a Jew from abroad who was also a Roman Citizen. They represented both groups of Jews—the Hebrews (Jews of Judaea) and the Hellenists (Jews from abroad). The letters gave them their authority. They would be able to give the decisions of the Council by word of mouth—for the spoken word was, in those days, much more highly regarded than the written word.

The church at Antioch received the decisions with great joy. Now all Christians were united. The Gospel could be preached to men of all nations. The whole Roman world lay before them. Paul was now free to become the great "apostle of the Gentiles".

JERUSALEM IN LATE NEW TESTAMENT TIMES

Paul's second missionary journey (A.D. 50-52)

It was not long before Paul was eager to be off again on his travels. His faith and energy and vision were boundless. In his mind he was already planning to take the Gospel to Rome itself—even further, to Spain in the furthest west, on the very edge of the known world.

But Paul was a practical man as well as a visionary. He was always thorough in the organisation of his churches. First, he made sure that his churches were set up in key towns. From them the Gospel could be spread to the towns and villages round about. Then he chose and appointed "elders" to be responsible for each church, copying the organisation of the Jewish synagogue. Again, he carefully revisited his churches to strengthen them in their Christian faith and their Christian life. Finally, when he was unable to visit them, he kept in touch with them by letters and by personal messengers.

Now we can see why Paul began his second missionary journey by revisiting the churches he had founded on his first journey. He intended to travel once again with his old friend Barnabas. But a quarrel arose between them. Barnabas wanted to take Mark, his young nephew, with them. Paul refused, for Mark had deserted them on their first journey. When they had reached the mainland of Asia Minor, after visiting Cyprus, he had gone back home to Jerusalem. He may have been frightened of the difficult and dangerous journey through the mountains. He may have been jealous of Paul who was taking the place of his uncle as leader of the party. He may have been simply homesick. Whatever the reason, he had left them, and Paul would not take a deserter with him. Neither he nor Barnabas would give way. They parted company,

17

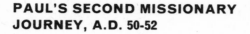

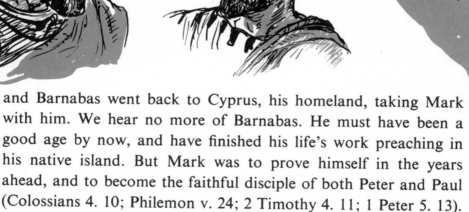

MACEDONIA

Thessaloni...

Berea

ACHAIA
(GREECE)

CORINTH

PAUL

SILAS

and Barnabas went back to Cyprus, his homeland, taking Mark
with him. We hear no more of Barnabas. He must have been a
good age by now, and have finished his life's work preaching in
his native island. But Mark was to prove himself in the years
ahead, and to become the faithful disciple of both Peter and Paul
(Colossians 4. 10; Philemon v. 24; 2 Timothy 4. 11; 1 Peter 5. 13).
And, of course, it is to Mark that we owe the very first Christian
gospel.

Paul chose Silas to accompany him, in place of Barnabas. Silas
is also known by the Roman form of his name, Silvanus, in the
New Testament letters (1 Thessalonians 1. 1; 1 Peter 5. 12). He
had been an early member and a leader of the church at Jerusalem.
He was a "prophet", an inspired preacher (Acts 15. 32). He had
been sent to Antioch to carry the decisions of the Council of

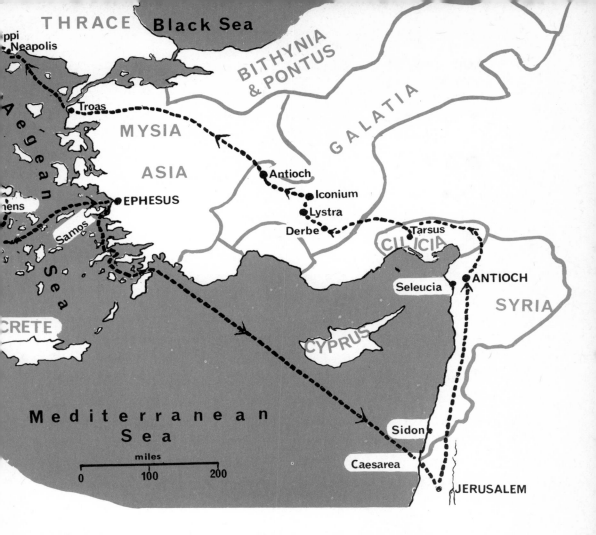

Jerusalem to the church there. He must have been thrilled by the
spread of the faith among Gentiles, for he had stayed on at
Antioch. Like Paul, he was dedicated to preaching to Gentiles.
He, too, was a Roman Citizen. He was an ideal companion for
Paul, in every way.

19

Timothy

Paul and Silas began their journey by land. They went northwards through Syria, visiting and strengthening the churches on their route. Then they made their way into Asia Minor through the famous mountain pass called the Syrian Gates. They must have passed two important towns on their way, though Luke does not mention them in his history book. One was Issus, where Alexander the Great had won his first victory over the Persians, centuries before, and so founded his Greek empire. The other was Alexandria, one of the many cities named after the all-conquering Greek, still known today as Alexandrette.

Paul's first aim was to visit the churches he had founded in his homeland of Cilicia, during the ten years he was working there before Barnabas took him to Antioch. He would certainly have visited his home town of Tarsus. Then, on from Tarsus, the missionaries went through the narrow passes in the Taurus Mountains known as the Cilician Gates. This was the famous, strategic highway used for thousands of years by armies marching between Asia Minor and Mesopotamia. Now they came out on to the plain where Paul had founded churches on his first missionary journey— at Derbe, Lystra, Iconium and Pisidian Antioch.

THE CILICIAN GATES
The Cilician Gates were deep, narrow defiles in the Taurus Mountains. Paul often used these narrow passes. Brigands made good use of them, as did armies throughout history.

At Lystra, Paul found a new disciple named Timothy, or, in the Roman form of his name, Timotheus. He had become a Christian during Paul's first visit to the town. Now Paul needed him as a secretary and assistant in his work. Timothy was the son of a Greek father, but his mother, Eunice, was a devout Jewess (2 Timothy 1. 5). Paul realised that strict Jews would make more trouble if he took a Gentile with him. He therefore had Timothy circumcised, so making him a full Jew. Timothy was to be of great help to Paul during the rest of his ministry. He calls Timothy his "dear son" (1 Corinthians 4. 17), and often refers to him in his letters. Timothy was with Paul, from now onwards, as he went round his churches, making known the decisions of the Council of Jerusalem.

Paul's next aim was to move further west in Asia Minor, into the Roman province called Asia. Ephesus, its great city, was his goal. But something happened to prevent him. Whatever this circumstance was, Paul saw in it the guidance of the Spirit of God. He therefore turned north-west, and came into the land of Mysia. Now he could have gone eastwards into the Roman province of Bithynia. But, once again, Paul could not feel the guidance of God in such an enterprise. Instead, he went on to the west and came to Troas.

Troas

Alexandria Troas, to give it its full name, was one of the chief ports of the Roman province of Asia. It is much more famous in history as Ilium, or Troy, whose story is told in the Iliad, the Greek epic written by the poet Homer. He told how ten years of war between the Greeks and the Trojans had ended in the destruction of Troy, made possible by the clever ruse of the "Trojan horse". The ruins of the legendary city lay near the town of Troas visited by Paul. Archaeologists have found there the remains of nine towns, buried beneath each other over the centuries. The earliest settlement there dated back to about 3,000 B.C.

Troas lay about ten miles from the Hellespont, the narrow channel separating Asia Minor from Europe, known today as the Dardanelles. The channel is between one and five miles wide. From Troas there were regular passages by sailing-ship to the Greek port of Neapolis. From Neapolis a famous Roman road ran right across Greece. It was the VIA EGNATIA, a paved highway that crossed Greece to the port of Dyrrhachium on the Adriatic Sea. From Dyrrhachium ships sailed regularly to Brundisium in Italy, and from Brundisium the famous Appian Way

led to Rome. Thus the Via Egnatia was the highway from Rome to the east.

Now we can understand why Paul had come to Troas. His strategy looked far beyond Asia Minor to the world of the west— to Greece, to Rome, even to Spain. An experience at Troas confirmed his intention. It seems that Paul fell ill at Troas, probably with his recurrent fever, for malaria may have been the "thorn in the flesh" that troubled him all his life. A Greek doctor was sent for. Paul, in his delirium, had what seemed to be a vision of a man of Greece saying, "Come over into Macedonia and help us." The Greek doctor stayed until Paul was recovered. In fact, he seldom left Paul again. His name was Luke and, from now onwards, in his story of Paul's travels, Luke speaks of WE, showing that he was with Paul.

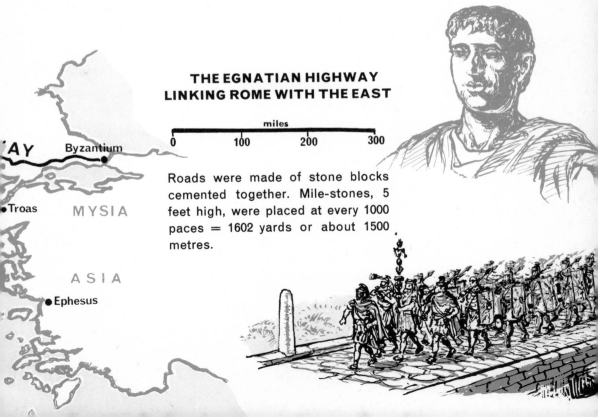

THE EGNATIAN HIGHWAY
LINKING ROME WITH THE EAST

miles

0   100   200   300

Byzantium

AY

Troas   MYSIA

ASIA

Ephesus

Roads were made of stone blocks cemented together. Mile-stones, 5 feet high, were placed at every 1000 paces = 1602 yards or about 1500 metres.

Philippi

The band of missionaries had grown in number. With Paul and Silas there were now Timothy and Luke. They sailed from Troas for Greece and, in two days, reached Neapolis, the terminus of the Egnatian Highway. Paul did not stay at tne port. He made straight for the great city of Philippi, ten miles further on.

Philippi was named after Philip of Macedon, father of Alexander the Great, who had conquered it in the fourth century B.C. The Romans had taken it in 168 B.C. The city was built on a height, and it was on the plains below the town that a great battle had been fought. Augustus, with Antony as his ally, had defeated the forces of Brutus and Cassius, the assassins of Julius Caesar. Their aim was to save the Roman republic from a dictator like Julius Caesar. The victory of Augustus at the battle of Philippi had set him on the road to power as Caesar Augustus, sole ruler of the whole Roman empire.

Augustus had commemorated his victory at Philippi by heaping privileges upon the town. It was made a Roman "colony", and veterans of the battle were settled there as "coloni". It was to become like another Rome, in the east. The citizens were given special privileges in ruling themselves, and this gave them civic pride. Their city prospered from the gold mines in the valley nearby. Philippi, as Luke says, had grown into "the chief city of that part of Macedonia" (Acts 16. 12). His pride in it strongly suggests that Luke himself came from Philippi.

The Egnatian Highway ran through Philippi. When archaeologists excavated the ruins, they found the ruts worn deep in the stone Highway by the wheels of countless chariots and waggons.

Over the Highway was a great arch and, a mile beyond it, the road crossed the narrow but swift river Gangites. It was here, by the river, that the Jews of Philippi met each sabbath day. It seems that there were not enough Jews to set up a synagogue of their own. By the river, outside the city, they had quietness and privacy, as well as water for their religious ceremonies. Among them was a woman named Lydia. She was a Gentile God-fearer, and came from the city of Thyatira in Asia Minor. She was engaged in the cloth trade, selling textiles dyed with the famous purple made from shellfish caught off the coast of Palestine. From it came the names Canaan ("Land of Purple") and Phoenicia ("Purple", in Greek).

Lydia was a prosperous business-woman, for only the very rich and the very powerful could afford to dress in purple robes. She had her own house in the town. Her independence shows the greater freedom of Gentile women as compared with the place of women among the Jews. Lydia was baptised into the Church, together with her household. She offered generous hospitality to the missionaries and persisted in her invitation until they agreed to stay at her house. It would have become the meeting-place of the church at Philippi. Women would have an important place in it.

THE MARKET-PLACE AT PHILIPPI

Paul and Silas imprisoned at Philippi

Lydia may have lived near the Forum, the centre of the life of the town. It was 300 feet long and 150 feet wide, and surrounded by public buildings and temples of the gods. On one side of the Forum was a raised stone platform, mounted by steps. It was here that the magistrates of the city sat to hear legal cases, and from here orators addressed the citizens. Paul and Silas were dragged before the magistrates at this very spot.

Paul had healed a girl with strange powers. The strange voice in which she cried out was believed to be the voice of a spirit or demon within her, possessing her. The Greek says that she had a "python"—the name of a dragon said, in the Greek myth, to have been slain by the god Apollo at Delphi. The word had come to mean what we should call a ventriloquist. The girl cried out after Paul and Silas. She sensed their spiritual powers. She used terms common among pagans, calling them servants of the "Most High God" who taught his "way of salvation", a term common in the popular Mystery Religions. Paul ordered the spirit to come out of her and, at least for a time, she became her normal self.

The girl's masters were angry when they saw that her powers were gone. They made good money from those who believed the girl to be inspired and paid to hear what the spirit spoke through her. They dragged Paul and Silas to the Forum, shouting and raising a mob. The crowd gathered before the magistrates, accusing Paul and Silas of being troublesome Jews, disturbing public order, and teaching customs contrary to Roman law. Jews were clearly unpopular in Philippi. The accusation was of using magic, in healing the girl, and that was certainly illegal. Both the magistrates

and the townspeople would be united in meeting any threat to their proud privileges as Roman citizens, living by Roman law. In the general uproar, Paul and Silas could not make themselves heard. They were given no chance to defend themselves. They were stripped and beaten and flung into the jail, just off the Forum. There, torn and bleeding, they were thrust in the stocks.

All this was a grave breach of justice. But it was even worse, for both Paul and Silas were Roman Citizens, protected by the imperial power. No one knew this, for there had been no trial, only mob violence before the magistrates themselves.

The jailor, accustomed to rough and brutal prisoners, was astonished to hear Paul and Silas singing hymns during the night. Then came the sudden earth tremor that shook the prison. The doors were closed by a wooden bar held in sockets on each door-post, and the bar would easily fall out with the movement of the posts. Shackles, too, came away from the walls. The jailor rushed in to secure his prisoners who might easily have dashed for freedom. He could not see Paul and Silas in the darkness of the inner dungeon where they had been secured. He was about to kill himself, thinking that they had escaped, knowing that his own life would be forfeit if they had. But Paul cried out that all the prisoners were there. The jailor took Paul and Silas into his apartment, tended their wounds and gave them food and drink. Overcome by their faith, he asked to hear the truth they proclaimed. That very night he and his household were baptised into the Church.

PAUL AND SILAS IN JAIL AT PHILIPPI

The Church at Philippi

The following morning the magistrates sent their officers with orders for Paul and Silas to be released. Paul refused to go. Two Roman Citizens had been submitted to mob violence, refused a fair trial, sentenced without being heard, publicly flogged, and shackled in jail. They were certainly not going to be pushed secretly out of the city. The magistrates were terrified when they heard of their appalling error. They hurried to the prison themselves, full of abject apologies, pleading with Paul and Silas to leave the city. Paul was satisfied with having taught them a lesson. It suited Luke's purpose, too, to describe this folly of minor local officials. It showed up, by contrast, the fairness of leading Roman administrators in their dealings with Christian missionaries accused before them.

Paul and Silas went to the house of Lydia, before leaving the city, to say goodbye to the group of Christians meeting there. Christians met in each other's houses, in the early years of the Church, for worship and fellowship. The house of a wealthy woman like Lydia would be large enough for their gatherings.

The cruel and illegal way in which Paul and Silas had been treated may well have won sympathy for their cause. They certainly left behind them a happy and warm-hearted group of Christian believers. Paul always looked upon the church at Philippi as his favourite. He was to visit Philippi again, as was his custom, and the New Testament preserves his letter, written to the Christians at Philippi, some ten years later. It is a happy letter, with scarcely a trace of problems or troubles among them. They helped Paul with gifts for his work and one of them, Epaphroditus, became his valuable and well-loved assistant (Philippians 2. 25).

Thessalonica

Paul and his companions continued along the Egnatian Highway from Philippi. Their first brief stop was at Amphipolis, 33 miles further on. It was an ancient Greek city, founded in the fifth century B.C. The Romans had made it the chief city of the district and given special privileges to its citizens. A further 28 miles brought the missionaries to Apollonia, named in honour of Apollo, the Greek god of the sun. Here too they did no more than rest for the night. For Paul's next goal was another key city—Thessalonica, 70 miles on from Philippi, and the chief seaport of Macedonia.

Salonica, as the town is known today, is still an important city, second only to Athens in size and importance. Thessalonica had been founded in 315 B.C. and named after the sister of Alexander the Great by her husband. It was a strategic centre, both by land and sea. It had a fine harbour and fertile land around it. The emperor Augustus had rewarded the city for its loyalty to him in his struggle for supreme power. It was made capital of the district, and a free city in which the citizens ruled themselves by their own laws. Its main street was the Egnatian Highway, and part of it is still so today. As at Philippi, too, it was spanned by arches. From the remains of one of these arches comes an inscription, today in the the British Museum, which refers to the city officials as "politarchs" ("rulers of the city"). This rare Greek word was the one used in Luke's history for the magistrates at Philippi who had treated Paul and Silas so badly. It is one of the many details which show us what a good historian Luke was.

THE EGNATIAN HIGHWAY, SPANNED BY ARCHES IN THE CHIEF CITIES WHICH IT PASSED THROUGH

The Church at Thessalonica

At Thessalonica, as at Philippi, the missionaries were brought before the politarchs, this time through the hostility of Jews. They had spent three weeks in the city, using the Jewish synagogue as their base for proclaiming the Gospel. A large commercial centre like Thessalonica naturally had a big Jewish colony. The Jews of the town were well-to-do. They had much influence, too, especially through the Gentile God-fearers who attended their synagogue. Paul and Silas won a few Jews by their preaching. But they had much greater success among the Godfearers who included leading women of the city.

Some Jews became jealous of the success of the Christian preachers. They got a band of ruffians to raise a riot against Paul and Silas. They assaulted the house of a Jew named Jason who had become a Christian, and who had given hospitality to Paul and Silas. Not finding the missionaries there, they dragged Jason and other believers before the magistrates. Christians were accused of disloyalty to the emperor, of proclaiming another king named Jesus, and of "turning the world upside down". The magistrates were troubled, but they released Jason and his companions on bail. Paul and Silas were the chief targets of Jewish hostility. They decided to leave the city secretly, by night, so that the church they had started could grow in peace. Jason himself was to prove a fine Christian leader, and we find him later with Paul at Corinth (Romans 16. 21).

Paul was to visit Thessalonica again to strengthen the church he had founded there. He kept in touch with it, too, by letters. Later, when he reached Corinth, he sent two letters to the church at Thessalonica. They are among the earliest of his letters in our New Testament. He had sent Timothy back to Thessalonica to carry on the work that he himself had been prevented from continuing. Timothy returned with encouraging news of the church there, but he reported some problems, too. Paul wrote to deal with them. Most members of the church were Gentiles. They had moral problems to face in making a complete break with their pagan past. There was also misunderstanding about the future life. The pagan world had little hope for life after death. Pagan funerals were times of sadness and despair. The Gentile converts had been thrilled by the Christian hope of eternal life. They were excited, too, at the prospect of the speedy return of Jesus to earth in his "second coming", a part of the early Christian preaching. Since they expected it to happen soon they even gave up their daily work. Paul wrote to correct such misunderstandings.

Athens

Paul and Silas, after their secret departure from Thessalonica, went on a further 50 miles to Berea—today the flourishing town of Verria. Here too there was a colony of Jews, and Paul naturally began his preaching in their synagogue. The Jews in Berea seem to have been quite unlike those in any other city that Paul had visited. They gave him a sincere welcome and a courteous hearing. They studied their sacred writings in an honest attempt to examine Paul's claims that all their prophecies had been fulfilled in Jesus. Many Jews came to believe. They were joined by Greek men and women in a new Christian group.

But peace was not to last. When the Jews of Thessalonica heard

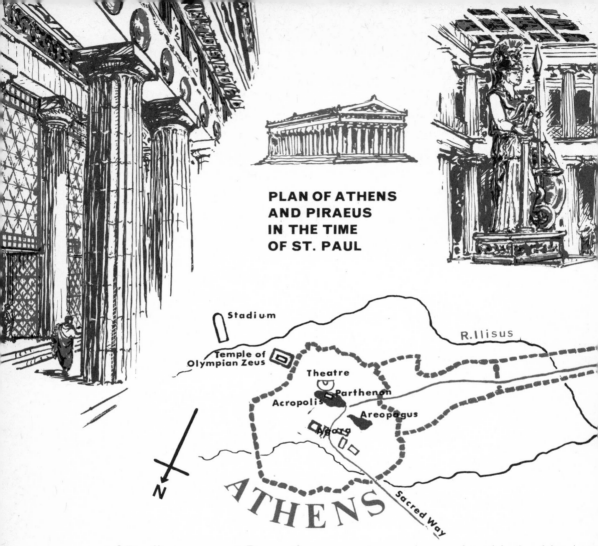

PLAN OF ATHENS
AND PIRAEUS
IN THE TIME
OF ST. PAUL

Stadium

R. Ilisus

Temple of
Olympian Zeus

Theatre

Parthenon

Acropolis

Areopagus

Agora

N

ATHENS

Sacred Way

of Paul's success at Berea they came to oppose and to hinder him in every way they could. They stirred up a mob at Berea, just as they had done at Thessalonica. Paul was the chief object of their attack. It was best for him to leave so that the work could go on peacefully. His safe departure was ensured by a clever ruse. It was made plain that Paul was going to leave by sea. Instead, his new Christian friends escorted Paul safely away by road. His goal now

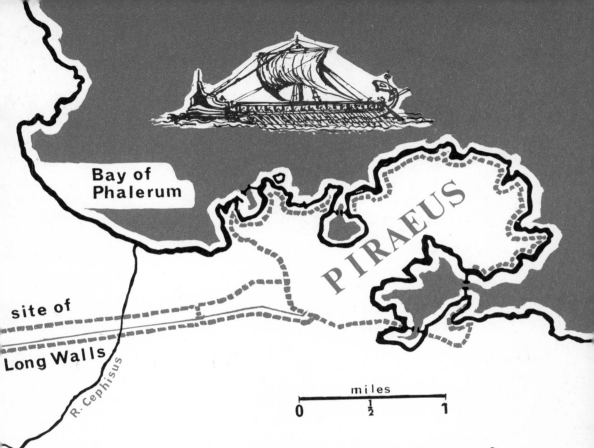

Bay of
Phalerum

PIRAEUS

site of

Long Walls

R. Cephisus

miles

0   ½   1

was the most famous Greek city of all—Athens, the home of
Greek philosophy and education. Paul's companions went with
him to Athens, far to the south. Then they returned to Berea with
instructions for Silas and Timothy to join Paul there.

We are not told that Paul had deliberately aimed to preach the
Gospel at Athens. Certainly it would have been a great achieve-
ment to have planted Christianity there, in the home of Greek
culture. Such a success would have won for Paul a hearing among
educated men throughout the Roman world. Perhaps this was his
strategy. In any case, Paul was never one to waste time, while he
waited at Athens for Silas and Timothy.

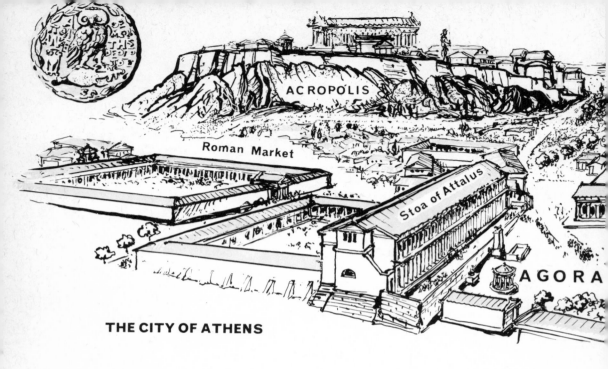

THE CITY OF ATHENS

The city of Athens

Athens had been at the height of its glory in the fifth century B.C. Such men as Socrates, Plato and Aristotle had made it the greatest centre of philosophy in the whole world. Now it was long past its glory. But Athens remained the home of wisdom and culture, famed in every land. Still today can be seen at Athens the glories of its civilisation in architecture and sculpture and art.

Piraeus, the port of Athens, was three miles from the city. The road between them was once enclosed by two walls, 200 yards apart. Along the road were altars to various gods, some of them not even named, and wayside shrines. Athens itself was a great religious centre, full of religious sanctuaries. The city was named after Athena, known to the Romans as Minerva. She was the

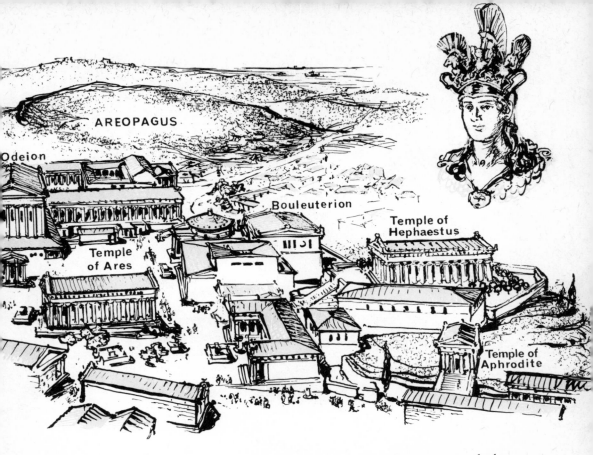

AREOPAGUS

Odeion

Bouleuterion

Temple of
Hephaestus

Temple
of Ares

Temple of
Aphrodite

goddess of wisdom, of war, and of the arts. The city surrounded
the ACROPOLIS or HIGH CITY, 512 feet high and dating from the
fifth century B.C. The Acropolis was approached through a splen-
did gateway. Within it were such magnificent buildings as the
temple of Wingless Victory (NIKE); the Erechtheum, a temple in
honour of the legendary king of Athens; and the great Parthenon,
temple of Athene. High above the Acropolis was a huge bronze
statue of the city's goddess. An ancient traveller wrote that sailors,
far out at sea, could see the sun glittering on her brazen spear
and helmet.

THE ACROPOLIS OF ATHEN

PARTHENON

ROMAN
TEMPLE

ERECHTHEUM

ALTAR
(A)

STATUE
of ATHENE

THEAT
DION

PROPYLAEA

TEMPLE
of NIKE

ROMAN
STEPS

40

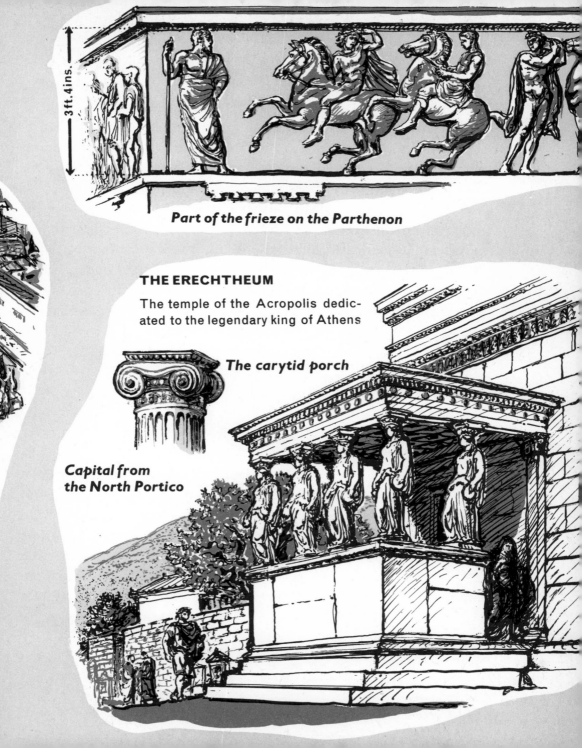

3 ft. 4 ins.

Part of the frieze on the Parthenon

THE ERECHTHEUM

The temple of the Acropolis dedicated to the legendary king of Athens

The carytid porch

Capital from the North Portico

The AGORA or MARKET-PLACE lies to the north of the Acropolis. American scholars have restored it, in recent years, spending a million dollars to bring to life the glory of ancient Athens. Athenians met in the agora to shop, to do business, above all to talk and to argue. Paul went each day into the agora, during his stay in Athens, entering into discussion with bystanders. This open space, surrounded by shops and shrines and public buildings, was the centre of city life. Among its surrounding buildings were the ODEION or Music Hall, the BOULEUTERION or Council Chamber, and temples dedicated to Apollo, Zeus, and the Mother of Gods. South of the Acropolis had been built the very first Greek Theatre for presenting the famous Greek dramas. South-east stood the greatest temple in all Greece, dedicated to Olympian Zeus. It stood over 90 feet high, and covered a site of 350 feet by 135 feet. The 15 columns which still stand suggest the magnificence of this glorious building.

The philosophers of Athens

Northwest of the Acropolis was the AREOPAGUS or HILL OF ARES. Ares was the Greek god of war known by the Romans as Mars, so that MARS' HILL was another name for the Areopagus. It is a bare hill about 375 feet high, but the remains of steps and seats, and of altars, too, can still be seen on its slopes. Here the city court sometimes met to hear legal cases and to discuss matters of politics and religion. It was here that Paul addressed a meeting of philosophers who had gathered to hear his teaching. They were mainly Stoics and Epicureans who had already come into contact with Paul in the marketplace. Paul, brought up in the university

Ares

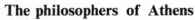

Areopagus

Hermes

town of Tarsus, was by no means ignorant of Greek culture and philosophy. Now an opportunity was made for him to expound his teaching.

Luke says that the Athenians were always on the look-out for anything new or novel. Paul's teaching was certainly novel, and he himself was no mean orator and thinker. The two words he was always using were "Jesus" and "Resurrection". "Jesus" was similar to the Greek verb meaning "to heal". Thus Jesus might be a god of healing. "Resurrection", ANASTASIS in Greek, would be his consort, a goddess.

Paul began his address by congratulating the Athenians on their religous devotion and piety. He spoke of an altar he had passed, on his way into the city. It had an inscription TO THE UNKNOWN GOD. This was quite natural in the ancient world. People believed in hosts of gods and goddesses. Some of them lived in the heavens, others were believed to dwell in certain places on earth, and others were seen in the forces of nature and in human virtues. All of them had supernatural power, it was believed. Sacrifices and prayers must be offered to win their favour and to keep away their ill-will. Every one had to be addressed by his or her correct name. To know the correct name of a god was to have power over him and to be sure of his favour. But there were hundreds of gods and even more names. To use the wrong name would be disastrous. That was why pagan worshippers used general terms when they were addressing a god, especially when they were not sure of its name. They would use an address such as "Whether thou be god or goddess" and "O unknown god". Such terms would cover every possibility.

Dionysus

Hera

Aphrodite

Poseidon

AN ALTAR DEDICATED TO UNKNOWN GODS
Found at Pergamon in Asia Minor.

Paul may have known this pagan custom. But he made the term "unknown god" serve as a text for his address. He was making God known—the one and only God, Creator and Lord of all, living and moving through all his creation. He was not shut up in temples. He was not to be located in idols made by men. He had revealed himself, made himself known, and now he called on men to turn to him. He had revealed himself in a man, Jesus of Nazareth, whom he had raised from the dead.

Paul's failure at Athens

The idea of a man being raised from the dead was indeed a novelty to the Greek philosophers. Some of them had a good laugh at such a fantasic idea, and mocked Paul. Others took him seriously, and wanted to meet again to discuss Paul's teaching further. A few believed. Among them was a woman named Damaris and a member of the Council named Dionysius.

Paul had tried to preach the Gospel at Athens in every way possible. He had spoken with the Jews in their synagogue; he had argued and discussed with the townsfolk in the market-place; now he had addressed the city's philosophers and leading men of the city. He had done his best to present the Gospel to these wise men in terms of their own wisdom. He had spoken, in his address, of Greek philosophy, poetry, sculpture, architecture, and religion. It had been a failure, and he had smarted at their mockery. He did not stay for another meeting with the philosophers. He made up his mind that never again would he try to present the Gospel in terms of men's wisdom. In a letter which he wrote shortly afterwards he vowed that he would preach nothing but "Christ crucified"—a stumbling-block to the Jews and foolishness to the Greeks (1 Corinthians 1. 17-27). The wisdom of God was all that mattered. It might well seem foolishness to sophisticated men of the world, proud of their own cleverness.

There is no evidence of a church being formed at Athens, nor of Paul revisiting the city, nor of him writing to Christians there. He must have felt, as he left, that his visit had been a grim failure. The last building he would see on the skyline was the wonderful Parthenon, temple of the heathen goddess of the city. Paul could not know then that, in years to come, the Parthenon itself would be used for Christian worship.

Corinth

Paul travelled on from Athens to Corinth, 40 miles to the west. In 146 B.C. the city had been destroyed by the Romans. But it had been rebuilt and made into a Roman colony by Julius Caesar in

46 B.C. Corinth had a wonderful position on a narrow isthmus, with two deep-water harbours, one on the east and the other on the west. It was thus a strategic centre for trade with both the world of the west and the world of the east. The emperor Augustus made Corinth the capital of the province of Achaia, the Roman name for Greece. This made it the seat of the Roman Proconsul and a great political centre.

Nothing could have been better for Corinth than a canal between its two harbours. This would have increased its trade with both east and west and made the city even more prosperous. Such a canal had often be planned in history—by Alexander the Great and by Julius Caesar, among others. Nero, the half-crazy emperor of Rome, had decided to construct a canal in A.D. 66. He himself had made the first cut in the earth with a golden spade. 6,000 Jewish prisoners had been brought from Palestine to toil on the vast undertaking. But local superstition hindered the work, and in time it was abandoned. It was not until modern times that the Corinth Canal was at last constructed, working to almost the same plan as Nero's. The twelve years of work ended in 1893 with the completion of the four mile canal. In the time of Paul, cargoes had to be carried over the isthmus from one harbour to the other. Small ships were even dragged overland with their cargoes on board.

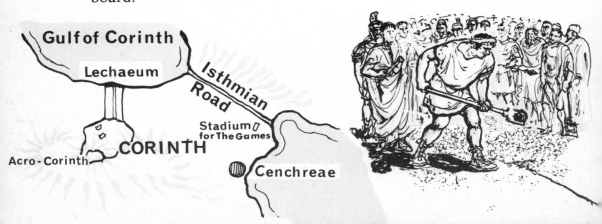

Gulf of Corinth

Lechaeum

Isthmian Road

Stadium for The Games

CORINTH

Acro-Corinth

Cenchreae

THE ISTHMIAN ROAD AT CORINTH

The City of Corinth

A great earthquake in 1858 led to the building of a new city of Corinth. Archaeologists were thus able to excavate the old city as they wished. They found that the road from Lechaeum, the harbour on the west, led into the AGORA or market-place. The business quarter lay off the Lechaeum Road, with shops opening on to the streets. It would be here that Paul worked at his trade of tent-making. On one side of the road, as it neared the market-place, was the civic building called a BASILICA (Greek "royal-house"). This was a great oblong hall, with two rows of stone pillars and an apse at the end, used as the law-court and for public assemblies. This plan of building basilicas was common throughout the Roman world. It was to be copied by Christians for their church buildings, divided by the columns into "nave" and "aisles".

Opposite the basilica was one of the many temples to Apollo. Under the neighbouring houses were found water-mains, as in our towns today. They brought fresh mountain water from the famous city springs. A marble stairway, spanned by a fine gateway, led into the agora. Here was found an inscription, carved in Greek letters—SYNAGOGUE OF THE JEWS. Near here must have been the synagogue in which Paul spoke week by week during his stay of 18 months at Corinth. Near here, too, must have been the house of Justus where he lodged, for Luke tells us that it "joined hard to the synagogue".

The market-place was lined by shops and temples, halls and porches, as in most cities. Under the shops were found storerooms and wells. The gutters were made of marble and the floors covered with mosaic designs. One stone block had been a door-step. Its inscription read LUCIUS THE BUTCHER. Here must have been the Meat Market to which Paul referred in a later letter to his church at Corinth (1 Corinthians 10. 25).

Paul before the Proconsul

One part of the open agora was raised eight feet. This raised platform was used on public occasions. Gallio the Proconsul sat here when giving judgement. It was here that Paul was brought before his judgement-seat.

MARKET STOA, CORINTH

Stoa   Well   Shops

The Jews had, as so often, grown hostile to Paul. They brought him before Gallio, accusing him of teaching men to worship God contrary to the law. They hoped to impress the Proconsul by a large delegation from their synagogue. They hoped, too, that Gallio would think that they accused Paul of breaking Roman law, when what they really meant was Jewish Law. Gallio was not to be taken in so easily. He was not a local magistrate but an imperial Roman. He was a well-born Roman from a distinguished family. His brother was Seneca, the great Stoic philosopher who had been tutor to the future emperor, Nero. The cultured and distinguished Proconsul was himself a man of high character.

Paul did not even have to speak in his defence. Once Gallio had heard the accusation, he quickly ended the matter. Had Paul been accused of any crime or of breaking Roman law there would have been a full trial. But this was a domestic dispute among Jews. Gallio had no official concern with Jewish Law. He refused to judge such a matter, and dismissed the Jewish delegation. This decision was popular with the crowd of Greeks in the agora. They were delighted to see leading Jewish citizens dismissed so curtly. To celebrate the occasion, and to show their feelings towards the Jews, they beat up Sosthenes, president of the synagogue. Strictly, Gallio should have dealt with them for mob violence and public disorder. He decided to turn a blind eye and ignored the affair.

The decision of Gallio was important for Christians. Luke purposely stresses it, in his history. It meant that Christians were regarded officially as a Jewish sect—protected, as all Jews were, by Roman Law. They were not a separate, and therefore illegal, group. Luke was always at pains to show the hostility of Jews and the friendliness of Roman officials to Christianity.

A Roman inscription, found at Delphi, refers to the Proconsul Gallio. It is a letter from the emperor Claudius and, in it, he refers to "Lucius Junius Gallio, my friend the Proconsul of Achaia". It was dated A.D. 52, and it shows that Paul must have reached Corinth about A.D. 50. This firm dating helps us to work out the chronology of Paul's life and journeys. It shows, too, how exact Luke was in writing his history.

Among the fine buildings near the agora was the Temple of Apollo. It was built in the sixth century B.C. and seven of its great columns still stand. Other temples were dedicated to Asklepios, the god of healing, and to the goddess Athene. High above the city stood the temple of Aphrodite, the goddess known as Venus to the Romans. People came to Corinth from many lands, bringing their gods with them. The great cosmopolitan city was full of their shrines and sanctuaries.

The great Theatre, where Greek plays were performed, seated 18,000 people. Near the theatre was found an inscribed stone block which had been part of a pavement. It recorded the name of a certain Erastus, the "aedilis" or official in charge of Public Works. It stated that he had provided the pavement at his own expense, in recognition of the honour of his office. Erastus became a Christian and an assistant of Paul. Paul refers to him in one of his letters as "oikonomos" or "steward" of the city—as we should say City Treasurer (Romans 16. 23). Erastus was thus a high official of the city of Corinth. His conversion is another example of important men and women entering the Church.

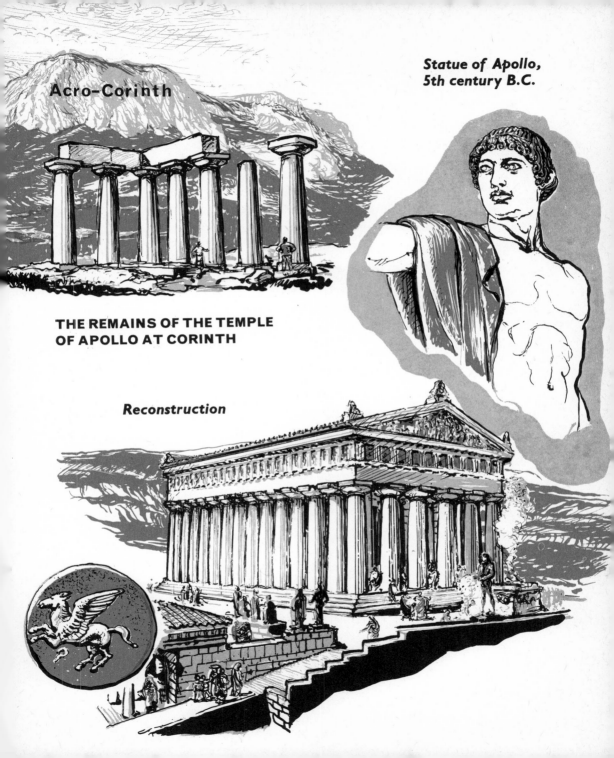

Acro-Corinth

Statue of Apollo,
5th century B.C.

THE REMAINS OF THE TEMPLE
OF APOLLO AT CORINTH

Reconstruction

Paul at Corinth

It was during his eighteen months at Corinth that Paul wrote his two letters to the church at Thessalonica, Timothy acting as his secretary. He was living with a married couple named Aquila and Priscilla. Aquila came from Pontus in Asia Minor. He had settled at Rome to follow his craft of tent-making. But in A.D. 49 the emperor Claudius had banished all Jews from Rome because of their constant rioting—caused, it seems, by the doctrine of Jesus as the Messiah being preached in their synagogues. Aquila and his wife had to leave Rome and they settled at Corinth. They were glad to have a skilled worker like Paul to help them in their business, weaving tent-cloth on their looms. It is probable that they had become Christians while they had lived at Rome. They were certainly members of the church at Corinth and they were devoted to Paul. They travelled on with him, after he left Corinth, helping him in his work.

Paul had settled in the Jewish colony at Corinth. He spoke each week in the synagogue to the assembled Jews and God-fearers. The theme of his preaching was, as always, that Jesus of Nazareth, spurned by the Jews, was the Messiah of God. The Jews rejected such teaching. Any man who died as a common felon on the cross must have been accursed by God, they replied. Paul became angry. With a dramatic gesture he cried out that he would leave them to their stubbornness. He would devote himself to Gentiles.

The church at Corinth

Paul won few converts among the Jews. But one of them was Crispus, the chief ruler of the synagogue, who was baptized together with his household. Sosthenes, his successor as president of the synagogue, was the Jew beaten up before the Proconsul. He too seems to have been sympathetic to Paul's preaching, and to have become a Christian, since he is mentioned by Paul in a letter to the church at Corinth (1 Corinthians 1. 1). But Paul had far greater success among the Gentile God-fearers. One of them, Titus Justus, probably a Roman, offered his hospitality to Paul. His house, next door to the synagogue, became the meeting-place of the Christians of Corinth. Another convert, as we saw, was Erastus the City Treasurer. Others mentioned are Gaius, and the household of Stephanas (1 Corinthians 16. 15).

INSCRIPTION MADE BY ERASTUS, CITY TREASURER OF CORINTH
An important official who became a Christian (Acts 19.22; Romans 16.23).

Paul may have had private money of his own. But he deliberately worked at his craft so as to mix with people and to have further opportunity for spreading the Good News. He entered fully into the life of the city, as he did in every town. He visited every part of it, mixing with both high and low. His letters, written later to the church at Corinth, show how well he knew the daily life of the town. He went with the crowds to the great Isthmian Games. He watched the dedicated athletes striving for victory in

53

their sports. He saw the boxers, with leather thongs wrapped round their knuckles, hammering their blows home. He saw the coveted wreath of withered celery placed on the head of each champion (1 Corinthians 9. 24-27).

Paul refers, too, to the law-courts where strict Roman justice was administered. Christians, he wrote, should settle their differences among themselves rather than seek justice from pagans, however fair they were.

Paul himself saw nothing wrong in buying and eating meat which had been part of a pagan sacrifice, or even in accepting an invitation to a pagan feast (1 Corinthians 8. 10). Both these actions would horrify strict Jews, and for that reason Paul abstained from them. He deliberately made himself "all things to all men" in order that he might win at least some to faith in Jesus.

Paul was also familiar with agriculture (1 Corinthians 9. 7-10). He must have had friends, perhaps converts, among the shepherds and farmers and landworkers. The vineyards of Corinth produced the famous grapes which gave us our word "currant"—a corruption of "Corinth". All these men were Gentiles and it was among them that the Church chiefly grew. But this brought special problems. The great cosmopolitan city of Corinth was filled with every pleasure and every vice. The popular saying, "to live like a Corinthian", meant to live for luxury and pleasure. Near the market-place was found a long colonnade, 100 feet long and 80 feet wide. Behind it were the night-clubs of Corinth—33 taverns where the people gave themselves over to pleasure. It was not easy for such gay and pleasure-loving people to change their way of life when they entered the Church. Paul had many problems to deal with in his letters to the church at Corinth. For, as was always his custom, he kept in touch with the church he had founded there, and visited it again when he was able.

The return to Antioch
Paul left Corinth by ship from its eastern harbour of Cenchreae. He had over 1,000 miles to travel back to his headquarters at Syrian Antioch. But his first goal was Jerusalem which he intended to reach in time for the Passover Feast. At Cenchreae he "made a vow", a symbolic act of gratitude to God. It was symbolised by shaving the hair grown during the thirty days of the vow and offering it in the Temple. Thus, Paul was in haste to reach Jerusalem.

55

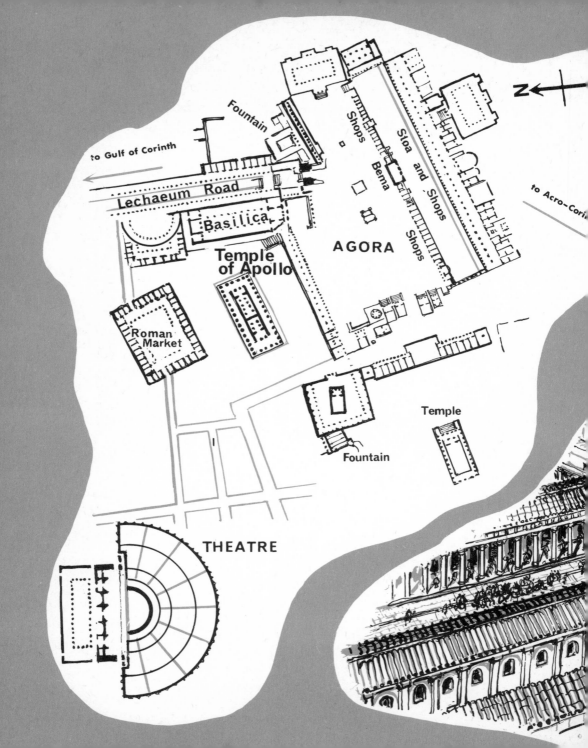

to Gulf of Corinth

Fountain

Shops

Stoa and Shops

Shops

Bema

Lechaeum Road

Basilica

Temple of Apollo

AGORA

to Acro-Cori

Roman Market

Fountain

Temple

THEATRE

PLAN OF THE CITY OF CORINTH

Feet
0 — 200

Remains of the Lechaeum Road leading to the Agora

The Agora looking south

He sailed 250 miles across the Aegean Sea to the great city of Ephesus in Asia Minor. It was the capital of the Roman province of Asia, rivalled only by the cities of Alexandria and Syrian Antioch in the eastern Mediterranean. It had long been Paul's ambition to preach the Gospel at Ephesus, but it was not to be fulfilled yet. It is possible that the ship only put in at Ephesus so that the Jewish pilgrims on board could attend the synagogue on the sabbath. Paul spoke in the synagogue, and he was pressed to stay. But he had to reach Jerusalem in time for the Feast, since he had made a vow. He promised that he would return.

Paul landed at Caesarea, the Roman port of Palestine built by Herod the Great. He travelled overland the 64 miles to Jerusalem. He kept the Feast there, as he had vowed. This visit to Jerusalem was uneventful. Leaving the city, he travelled north by land to his base at Syrian Antioch. There he would spend the winter when travelling was difficult.

Paul must have received a great welcome from the church at Antioch. He had much to tell. This second missionary journey had lasted from A.D. 50 to 52. It had taken the Gospel to Europe and planted churches in the key cities of Macedonia and Greece. From them it would spread out further still.

To find and read in your Bible

Paul on the road to Damascus	Acts 9. 1-30
Paul's first missionary journey	Acts 13. 4—14. 28
The Council of Jerusalem	Acts 15. 6-35
Paul and Barnabas quarrel	Acts 15. 36-40
Timothy joins Paul	Acts 16. 1-3
Paul revisits the churches of Asia Minor	Acts 16. 4-6
Paul's vision at Troas	Acts 16. 8-10
Paul at Philippi	Acts 16. 11-15
Paul and Silas imprisoned at Philippi	Acts 16. 16-40
Paul at Thessalonica	Acts 17. 1-10
Paul at Berea	Acts 17. 10-14
Paul at Athens	Acts 17. 16-34
Paul at Corinth	Acts 18. 1-18
Paul returns to Antioch	Acts 18. 18-22

To map

Make your own map of this second missionary journey of Paul in Asia Minor and Europe.

To research

Use reference books to find out all you can about Roman roads, especially how they were made. Tell the story of one particular road. It may be the Egnatian Highway, or the Appian Way, or you may prefer to tell the story of Roman roads in Britain— especially any near your home.

To report

Imagine that you were a newspaper reporter in Philippi. Write an account of the visit of Paul and Silas, and all that happened.

59

Corn being loaded on to
an Egyptian grain-ship
from a painting at Ostia, c.A.D.
50

A GLOSSARY OF TYPES OF BUILDINGS IN THE TIME OF ST. PAUL

Greek Temple

Roman Temple

Greek Agora

Houses

Triumphal Arch

Roman Forum

Stoa

Stadium for athletic contest

Gymnasium for training athletes

Hippodrome for chariot racing

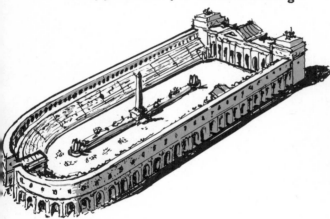

Amphitheatre for gladitorial and animal contests

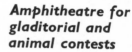

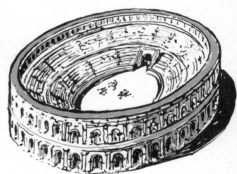

Roman Theatre

Greek Theatre

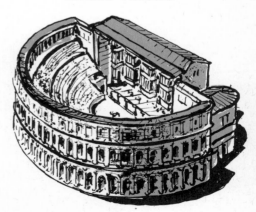

To imagine

Imagine that you were the son or daughter of the jailer at Philippi, living in the jailer's house. Tell the story of the two prisoners, Paul and Silas, and what happened during their stay.

To compose

From these references, in Paul's letters to his church at Thessalonica, make up an address which Paul might have given:

God is our Father	1 Thessalonians 1. 3
Jesus is his Son	1 Thessalonians 1. 10
Jesus died for all	1 Thessalonians 5. 10
He rose from the dead	1 Thessalonians 4. 14
He brings salvation	1 Thessalonians 5. 9
Jesus will return	1 Thessalonians 4. 16
Christians must live by faith, love and hope	1 Thessalonians 1. 3
Christians must discipline themselves	1 Thessalonians 4. 3
Christians must do honest work	2 Thessalonians 3. 12
Christians must live in peace	1 Thessalonians 5. 13

To research

Use reference books and travel guides to make a personal booklet or a class frieze of ancient Athens.

To draw

Use reference books to find plans of a "basilica", copied by Christians for churches. Draw one, to show the plan of the building, and show how the rows of pillars made what we call "nave" and "aisles" in a church building.

To letter and remember

Here are some fine passages from Paul's letters for you to letter in illuminated writing, or to write out, to help you to remember them:

Peace: Romans 15. 13   Kindness: Ephesians 4. 32 and 5. 1-2

Joy: Philippians 4. 4-6   Generosity: 2 Corinthians 9. 6-7

To design

Design a letter-card for one of the cities mentioned in this chapter. It will consist of pictures of the main sights of the town for visitors to buy to send to their friends back home. You may choose Philippi, or Athens, or Corinth. Draw or paint the chief glories of the city.

To model

Use reference books to help you to model a typical city of the time of Paul. You may choose one of the cities described in this chapter, or make a general model of a Greek city.

To imagine

Imagine that you were Timothy, leaving home at Lystra to journey with Paul as his secretary. Write a letter home to your mother, Eunice, telling her of your adventures with Paul on his travels.

To act

Paul lived and worked with his friends, Aquila and Priscilla, at Corinth. Act a scene between these three. They will have their work as tent-makers to discuss, but also their much more important work for the Church.

The Church in Asia Minor and Europe

Paul's third missionary journey (A.D. 52-56)

Paul was a brilliant organiser, as well as a powerful preacher. It was always his careful strategy to revisit the churches he had founded, so as to strengthen them in their Christian faith and life; and, in between his visits, to keep in touch with them by messengers and letters. His second missionary journey had begun by revisiting churches; and, during it, he had written letters which we can still read in our New Testament. His third missionary journey was to have exactly the same pattern.

Paul spent the winter at Syrian Antioch, his headquarters. In the new year he set off again. He took with him a group of young men who had become Christians during his earlier missions. They would help Paul in his work, acting as secretaries and messengers. But they had been specially chosen for their Christian faith, their characters, and their abilities. They were not simply Paul's assistants. He was training them to become leaders in the Church after him. They included Timothy from Lystra; Titus, probably from Antioch; and Erastus, the former City Treasurer of Corinth.

This third missionary journey was to be the longest yet, lasting four years. It was to take Paul through Asia Minor and through Greece. He began by travelling north by land from Syrian Antioch into Cilicia, revisiting the churches he had founded there ten years before. The missionary party then went into the Roman province of Galatia through the mountain passes, the famous Cilician Gates. There Paul went round the churches he had founded on his first missionary journey—at Derbe, Lystra, Iconium and Pisidian Antioch.

Now came a new and important venture. For a long time Paul had wanted to plant the Gospel in the great city of Ephesus, in the west of Asia Minor. On his previous journey he had been turned

away from his goal by some circumstance in which he had seen the guidance of God. On the voyage back, his ship had put in briefly at Ephesus—perhaps for the party of Jewish pilgrims on board to keep the sabbath in the synagogue there. Paul had naturally spoken in the synagogue that day, and he had been asked to stay. But his plan to reach Jerusalem for the Passover Feast had prevented him staying longer. He had promised to return. Now the time had come.

66

It was not simply a matter of keeping a promise that brought Paul back to Ephesus. It had always been his strategy to plant churches in the great cities of the world. They were key centres from which the Gospel would spread out to neighbouring towns and villages. Ephesus was one of the greatest cities in the Mediterranean, rivalled only by Alexandria and Syrian Antioch. It was a key city in Paul's missionary strategy.

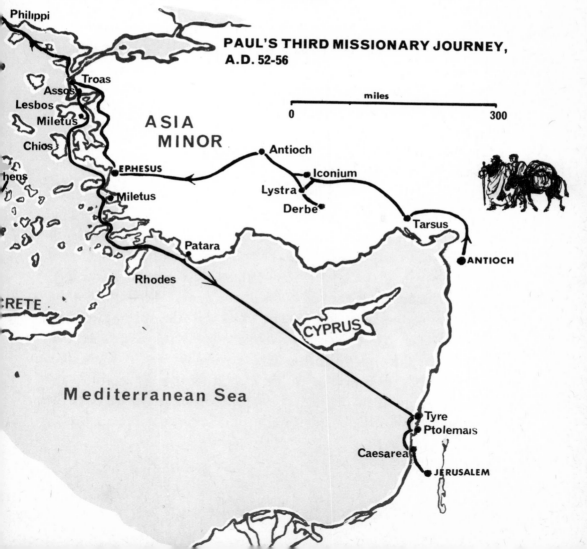

PAUL'S THIRD MISSIONARY JOURNEY, A.D. 52-56

Philippi

Troas

Assos

Lesbos

Miletus

Chios

ASIA MINOR

EPHESUS

Miletus

hens

miles

0   300

Antioch

Iconium

Lystra

Derbe

Tarsus

ANTIOCH

Patara

Rhodes

CRETE

CYPRUS

Mediterranean Sea

Tyre

Ptolemais

Caesarea

JERUSALEM

Ephesus prepared for the Gospel

Paul's brief earlier visit to Ephesus (Acts 18. 19-21) had helped to prepare the way for the long ministry there which he now intended. But there had been other helpers, too. Among them had been Aquila and Priscilla, a married couple with whom Paul had lived and worked at Corinth. Being tent-makers, they could work at their craft and find business in any great city. They had lived previously at Rome, until driven out by the emperor's edict banishing all Jews from the city. At Corinth they had helped Paul greatly in his missionary work, as well as providing him with a home and livelihood. When he had sailed from Corinth, on his return journey, they had journeyed with him. They had left the ship at Ephesus and had settled there. Their home at Ephesus had become the meeting-place of devout men and women of the city. Their witness to the Christian faith had helped to prepare the way for Paul's coming.

To Ephesus, also, had come a Jew from Alexandria named Apollos. The city of Alexandria in Egypt was a great centre of Greek culture. It had, too, a large colony of Jews of the Dispersion. Some were wealthy merchants who organised the corn trade between North Africa and Rome. Others were scholars, and from them had come the Greek version of the Jewish Scriptures which we know as the Septuagint. The Jews of Alexandria were, of course, Hellenists—Jews who spoke the Greek language and followed the Greek way of life. The Jewish scholars of Alexandria studied Greek philosophy in this great centre of culture and learning. From them came a new type of Judaism which wove together Jewish beliefs and Greek philosophy. It found hidden meanings in Bible stories by interpreting them as allegories. Paul himself sometimes used allegories. For example, he describes a Roman soldier, in one of his letters, making every part of his equipment into a Christian symbol (Ephesians 6. 13-18).

Apollos was one of these Jewish scholars from Alexandria. He was a cultured, well-educated Jew, with a brilliant mind and a wonderful gift of oratory. He had heard of the preaching of John the Baptist, the herald of Jesus. John had proclaimed the coming of the Messiah, and Apollos had been inspired by this great hope. He was what we might call a "half-Christian". When he came to Ephesus, he spoke with great power in the synagogue. But his understanding of the Christian faith was not complete. He did not know how the prophecies of John had been fulfilled in Jesus. Aquila and Priscilla took him into their home, and instructed him in the faith which they had learnt from Paul. Now he could interpret the Jewish Scriptures to show how they had been fulfilled in Jesus.

Apollos had left Ephesus before Paul arrived there. He went on to Greece and became a powerful Christian preacher there, skilful in discussions with Jews over the meaning of their Scriptures. He became so popular in the church at Corinth that Christians there divided into rival groups. Some called themselves followers of Paul, and others formed the party of Apollos. Apollos never intended this. It happened because some thought his brilliant preaching far better than that of Paul, and they looked to him as their leader. Paul was horrified when he heard of this rivalry. In a letter to the church at Corinth he taught the evil of such divisions within the family of God (1 Corinthians 1. 12-13; 3. 5-6).

We hear no more of Apollos. Some think that he was the author of the Letter to the Hebrews in the New Testament. Certainly its author wrote the purest Greek, and he was a Jew who was familiar with Greek philosophy, as well as with the teachings of Paul. Paul himself never made any attempt to visit Alexandria, although he carefully planted churches in the two other great Mediterranean cities of Syrian Antioch and Ephesus. Perhaps he deliberately left Alexandria to the ministry of Apollos, whom he trusted and admired (1 Corinthians 16. 12). Apollos, for his part, had certainly helped to prepare the way for Paul's ministry at Ephesus.

The city of Ephesus

Ephesus was the capital city of the Roman province of Asia. It had a population of over 250,000 people, making it the largest city that Paul had yet visited. It lay three miles from the sea, to which it was linked by the river Cayster. Even in Paul's time the silt, which has now blocked up the river, sometimes made it difficult for large

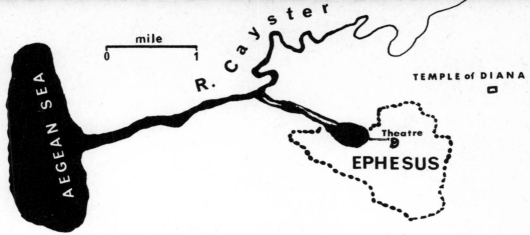

ships to sail up-river to Ephesus. Instead, they used the nearest port at Miletus. From Ephesus, highways led up into Asia Minor and away to the east. Thus the city was a great commercial link between east and west, as well as the market of Asia Minor. From commerce came the great wealth of Ephesus.

Ephesus had been linked in history with such famous names as Croesus of Lydia, Cyrus of Persia, and Alexander the Great. Its population was a mixture of Greeks with peoples of Asia Minor. When the Romans took over the city, about 190 B.C., they made it a free city. The citizens ruled themselves through their assembly.

Excavations began at Ephesus in 1863, and all the main buildings of the ancient city have been uncovered. It had the usual market-square, called the "agora" by the Greeks and the "forum" by the Romans. It was surrounded by civic buildings and temples and by colonnades for shops. The main street, later known as the "Ar-kadiane", ran between the theatre and the harbour. It was 1,735 feet long and paved with marble. On either side of the roadway, 36 feet wide, were colonnades with shops behind them. A fine arched gateway spanned the road where it entered the harbour.

71

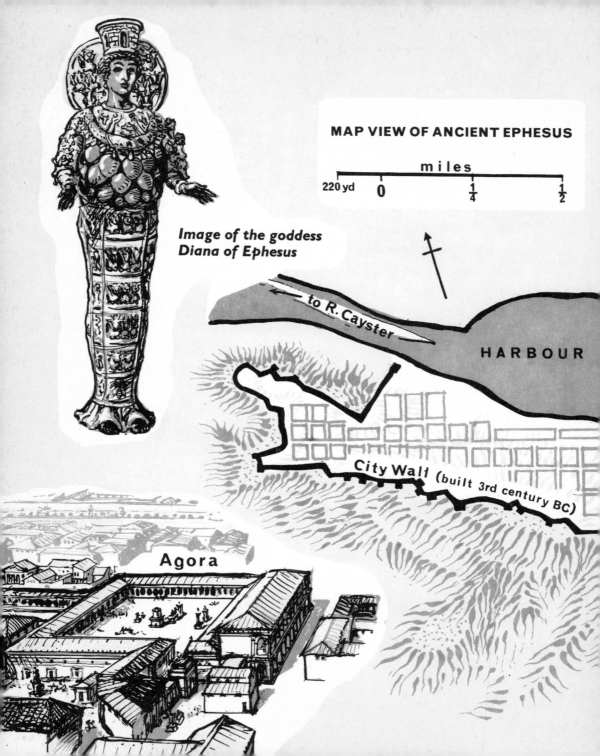

Image of the goddess
Diana of Ephesus

MAP VIEW OF ANCIENT EPHESUS

miles

220 yd   0   1/4   1/2

to R. Cayster

HARBOUR

City Wall (built 3rd century BC)

Agora

Theatre

Temple of Diana

Stadium

Mt. Pion

Theatre

Arkadiane

Agora

Council House

Gymnasium

Magnesian Gate

Fountain

Aqueduct

DIAN EPHE

"Ephesian Writings"

Ephesus was not only a great political and commercial centre. It was also famous as a centre of religion. Peoples of many races had come to Ephesus, bringing their gods and their superstitions with them. The mixed population of the city had become famous for their magic and spells and incantations. Such superstitious people were ready to believe in anything. Many made a good living by claiming to be "exorcists", driving out evil spirits. They used the saying I ADJURE YOU BY.... in addressing the spirit or demon with their magic formula (Acts 19. 13). Such men kept secret scrolls containing their magic spells.

Inscriptions, found on the walls of the ruined buildings of Ephesus, show how superstition flourished in the city that Paul knew. One of them read:

IF THE BIRD IS FLYING RIGHT TO LEFT,
AND SETTLES OUT OF SIGHT,
GOOD LUCK WILL COME.
BUT IF IT LIFTS UP ITS LEFT WING,
THEN, WHETHER IT RISES OR SETTLES OUT OF SIGHT,
MISFORTUNE WILL COME.

No wonder that Greek and Roman writers used the term "Ephesian Writings" for all magic spells and incantations.

Diana of the Ephesians

Ephesus was famous, most of all, for its cult of the great goddess called Artemis by the Greeks and Diana by the Romans. But the cult was much older than both peoples. It had begun in the eighth

74

century B.C. with a meteorite, believed to have fallen "from heaven". The goddess was the Great Mother, the nature goddess of fertility, bringing increase to both men and animals. She was identified with the rough stone image, and was worshipped where it fell with an altar and a sacred tree. Temples were, in time, built on the site, which was first discovered in 1869. The remains of five temples were found.

The fourth temple had been partly paid for by the fabulously rich king, Croesus of Lydia, where gold flowed in the mountain streams. It had taken over 100 years to build, and it had been one of the Seven Wonders of the ancient world. Dedicated about 425 B.C., it had been destroyed by fire in 356 B.C. The fifth temple had been begun about 350 B.C. and Alexander the Great, who visited the city twenty years later, paid for its completion. It had been designed by Dinocrates, the famous architect of Alexandria. It was this wonderful Greek temple that was the glory of Ephesus when Paul visited the city, and which was to stand until destroyed by the Goths in A.D. 262.

The worship of the Great Mother, the fertility goddess of nature and of man, was common all over the east. The people of Phoe-

nicia and of Canaan, for example, had worshipped such a goddess The Jews, when they entered the Promised Land of Canaan, had been tempted to worship her too. The goddess had been worshipped at Ephesus long before the rise of the Greeks. She was very different from their Artemis, the Roman Diana, who was the pure goddess of hunting and sister of the sun-god Apollo. But it was natural and common, in a world of many gods and goddesses, to identify one with another.

Ephesus was the "temple-keeper" or "warden" of the goddess— an honour which the citizens guarded jealously. Not only was she their supreme goddess. Her cult also brought them both fame and profit. Diana was worshipped throughout the world, and pilgrims came from near and far to worship at the sacred shrine of the goddess. They bought statues of the goddess, according to what they could afford, made of silver, terra-cotta, bronze, gold, ivory and wood. Making the images was an important local industry, especially for the guild of silversmiths.

Images of the goddess were modelled on the great statue of the goddess in the temple. She had her arms outstretched, a crown upon her head, and her body clad in a tight-fitting dress. Four rows of pendants hung on her front. They may have been orna-ments, but some think that they were breasts to symbolise the great goddess of fertility. Her dress was covered with images of other sacred beings, such as sphinxes and nymphs, and with rows of shells, bees, and roses. The top of her dress, or breast-plate, was covered with the signs of the zodiac. These would symbolise the link between the nature goddess and the seasons of the year which determined the life of agriculture.

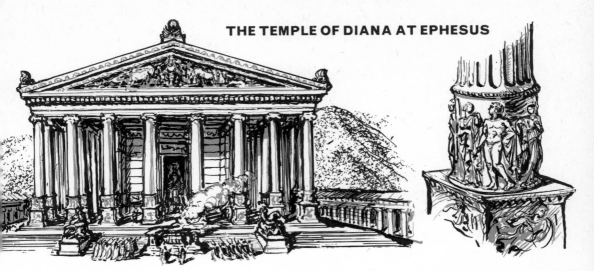

The temple was the centre of a great tourist industry. Pilgrims brought gifts to the temple. They paid to share in the religious festivities, some of which were crude and immoral. They bought images of the goddess and other souvenirs and charms. Pilgrims flocked to Ephesus for the annual ARTEMISION, the festival of the goddess held in March-April. The packed city enjoyed religious processions, when the statue of the goddess was drawn through the streets by deer—symbols of Diana often used on Greek coins.

But the focus of the festival was the temple itself. The temple area was 240 feet wide and 420 feet long. The temple building was 340 feet long and over 160 feet wide. It was supported by 100 sculptured columns, each 55 feet high, made of jasper. Behind the main altar, 20 feet square, was the statue of the goddess which, to her worshippers, had "fallen from heaven" (Acts 19. 35). The roof was covered with white marble tiles. Sculptures, vivid paintings and glittering gold made the temple one of the most beautiful buildings in the Roman world.

77

Paul at Ephesus

We saw how Apollos, the scholarly Jew from Alexandria, had helped to prepare the way for Paul's coming to Ephesus. Paul met some of his followers soon after his arrival, about a dozen in all. Apollos had made known to them the teaching of John the Baptist, and they shared his hope of the coming of the Messiah. They had been baptised, as John had bidden, and their hearts were ready for the kingdom of God. But, like Apollos, they were "half-Christians". They knew nothing of baptism in the name of Jesus, and of the Holy Spirit, giving power to those who believed. Then Paul showed them how John had been a herald, preparing the way for the far greater one who would come after him. He had come in Jesus of Nazareth. Jesus offered the power of his Spirit to those who believed in him and entered his family by baptism. On hearing this, the followers of Apollos gladly asked for baptism in the name of Jesus and, with the laying on of hands, the power of the Spirit came upon them. Thus Paul completed the work of Apollos.

Paul began his ministry, as was his usual custom, by speaking in the synagogue of the Jews. He spoke there for three months. This was a longer period than he had spent in any synagogue, but he was no more successful than in other cities. Hostility grew against him, at his preaching of Jesus the crucified Messiah—and probably jealousy, too, at his success with God-fearers.

Paul gave up the hopeless task. He hired a "school"—Greek SCHOLE—that is, a lecture hall, belonging to a teacher named Tyrannus. One manuscript of the New Testament adds that Paul taught there from the 5th to the 10th hour, the hottest part of the day between late morning and early evening. The working day began at sunrise, and Paul himself worked at his own trade from sunrise to the fifth hour, our 11 a.m., when work ceased. The lecture-hall would be used by Tyrannus during these hours, and again in the cool of the evening. Paul used it when it was not needed—during the fierce heat of the day.

Paul also talked with people in the market-place and in their homes. He did not attack the worship of Diana. He simply proclaimed the Good News of Jesus, during his two years of teaching in the lecture-hall. Paul, aided by his assistants, won many to the Christian faith. Faith in magical power was so great, among the people of Ephesus, that some believed they were healed by any piece of cloth which Paul had actually touched. Others, tired of their slavery to superstition and magic and belief in demons, found release in Christianity. They openly confessed their secret charms and spells. They gladly burnt their scrolls of magic formulas. Christianity brought light and hope into their dark world of superstition and fear.

THE FORUM AT EPHESUS, WITH SILVERSMITHS' SHOPS

Paul and the silversmiths

Paul had spent over two years at Ephesus, his longest stay in any city. It was time to move on to Greece and to revisit his churches there, set up on his second missionary journey. He was also talking openly, now, of going on from Greece to Rome. He sent Timothy and Erastus on ahead of him. He himself intended to stay on at Ephesus for a time. He believed that "a great door was opened" to him there (1 Corinthians 16. 9). The great annual festival of Diana was approaching. Ephesus would be packed with pilgrims from all over Asia Minor and beyond. It would be a wonderful opportunity to proclaim the Gospel.

Someone else saw his opportunity at the Festival of Diana, too. This was Demetrius, a silversmith. Trade had been dwindling for some time now, in the city, as a result of Paul's preaching. Paul had never openly attacked the worship of Diana. But two years of his preaching, that "they be no gods which are made with hands", were having their effect. Demetrius called the guild of silversmiths together and spoke his mind. It did not take him long to work them up, playing on their fears and touching them where it hurt most. Of course they could piously pose as champions of the goddess Diana, whose worship was threatened by Paul's preaching. But, as before at Philippi, it was when men's pockets were affected that they broke out into active hostility.

Demetrius and his fellow-craftsmen rushed out into the street shouting their battle-cry: GREAT IS DIANA OF THE EPHESIANS. The crowds quickly gathered. Demetrius led them in a vain hunt for Paul. The only Christians he could lay hands on were two Greeks named Gaius and Aristarchus. He and his fellows dragged

80

them towards the theatre, the mob following. The theatre was the public meeting-place of the populace. It had been constructed on the slope of Mount Pion, looking down on the city. The theatre seated 25,000 people, the seats rising tier on tier, and it was almost 500 feet in diameter. Still today can be seen the remains of seats, stage and orchestra, as well as of the statues which decorated the theatre.

In the theatre at Ephesus

Paul was intent on going to the theatre himself to reason with the mob, in spite of the dangers for him above everyone else. He was persuaded to stay away, however, by urgent appeals from the friendly ASIARCHS. They were Roman officials whose chief duty was to organise the rites and games and festivals in honour of the emperor. Emperor worship was a Roman device for binding together all the peoples of their vast empire under one sublime figurehead. Some emperors took it much more seriously than others. People in the east took it much more seriously than people in the west. Those in charge of fostering the imperial cult were important officials. Once again Luke brings out the friendliness of Roman officials to Paul and to Christianity. The Asiarchs may also have seen in Paul an ally in their efforts to weaken the cult of Diana so as to strengthen the cult of the emperor. It seems that an Asiarch retained his honorary title after his year of office had ended. That would explain the presence of a number of Asiarchs at the festival of Diana, the great event of the civic year, much as they may have disliked it.

The packed theatre was in an uproar. Many were not sure what all the fuss was about. But there was general awareness of some threat to the great goddess of the city. The slogan GREAT IS DIANA OF THE EPHESIANS was taken up by everyone in time, and Luke says that the mob chanted it for two hours.

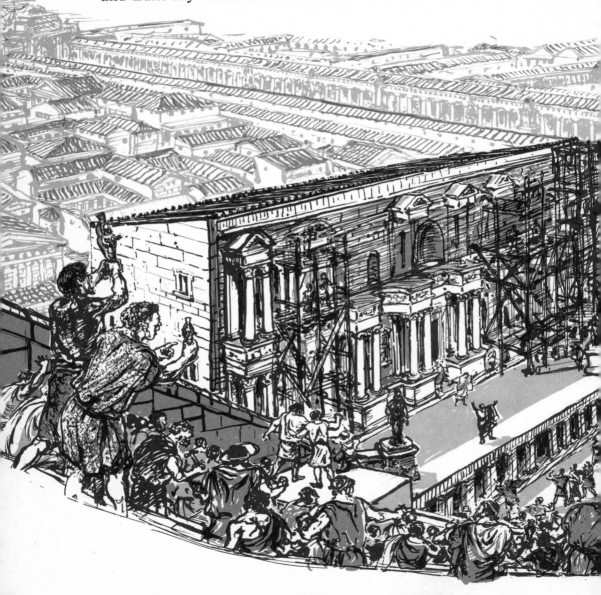

THE THEATRE AT EPHESUS
A reconstruction of the assembly of silversmiths and citizens

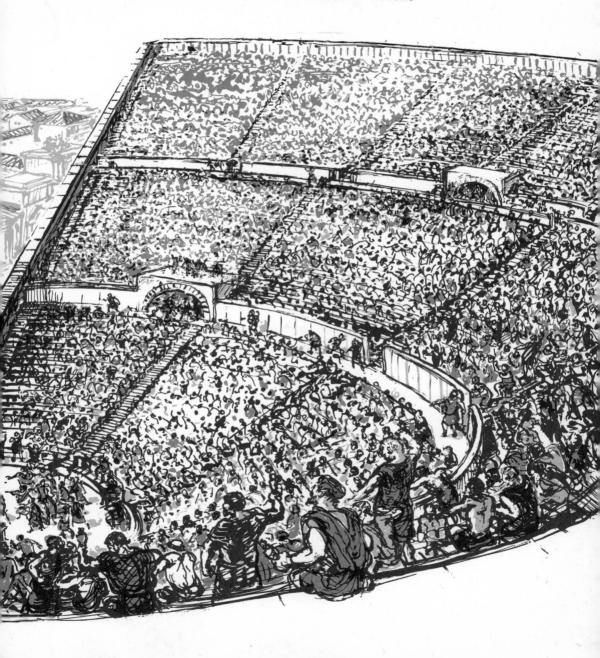

When the "town clerk"—the chief official of the city—came hurrying to the theatre, and called for silence, the crowd may well have been exhausted enough to listen. His words were tactful but firm. Everyone was well aware that the city of Ephesus was the temple-keeper of Diana, he pointed out. There was no need to shout about it in a public riot. The Christians had not robbed any temples, neither had they blasphemed against Diana. Demetrius and his fellowcraftsmen knew perfectly well that the courts and magistrates were available to settle all disputes, and that Roman law provided adequately for redress if their trade had been wronged. If there was any other matter it should be brought up at the regular public assembly. That was the proper occasion for public affairs—not this mob gathering. There were fixed dates for meetings of the assembly, as everyone knew. An extraordinary meeting could only be held by permission of the Roman authorities. They were always reluctant to give it, for their constant concern was public order. There was no excuse, therefore, for this disorderly affair. The sooner it was ended the better. The town clerk advised everyone to go home quickly and quietly, if they wanted to keep their privileges of self-government.

The wise words of the town clerk were taken to heart by the people of Ephesus, and they soon dispersed. But Paul realised that he was the target of the silversmiths. It would be best if he left the city, so that the church there could go on growing in peace. He had his plans to visit Greece, too. He left Ephesus shortly after the riot.

Churches of the Lycus valley

Luke concentrates upon the work of Paul in his history of the early Church. He does not tell us about the work of Paul's assistants. But we have seen that Paul chose to work in key cities so that the Gospel could be spread from them to neighbouring towns. This was exactly what happened as a result of his ministry at Ephesus.

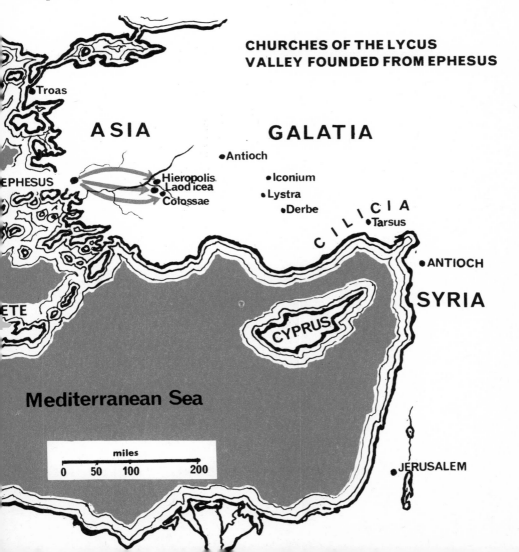

CHURCHES OF THE LYCUS VALLEY FOUNDED FROM EPHESUS

In the eastern part of the Roman province of Asia lay three important towns, all in the valley of the river Lycus. Paul may have passed through this valley on his way to Ephesus, but he did not stop to preach in these towns. Instead, while he was working at Ephesus, he sent his assistants to them. The three towns were Colossae, Laodicea and Hierapolis. One of Paul's assistants, named Epaphras, had himself come from Colossae.

Two letters of Paul in our New Testament were sent to these towns. One was his "*Letter to the Colossians*". It was written later when Paul was a prisoner, probably at Rome. It was to be read in the churches of Laodicea and Hierapolis, as well as in the church at Colossae. It was taken to Colossae by Tychicus (Colossians 4. 7-8) whom Paul calls a "beloved brother", and who himself came from Asia.

Another Christian went with Tychicus to Colossae, bearing a second letter. His name was Onesimus, which meant "Helpful", but he had not lived up to his name. He was a runaway slave whom Paul had found in great need. Paul had befriended him and helped him, and Onesimus had been baptised into the Church. Now he was going back to his master, Philemon, a wealthy citizen of Colossae. Paul had armed him with his "*Letter to Philemon*". He asked Philemon to receive back Onesimus just as he would have received Paul himself—as a Christian brother. For Philemon had become a member of the church at Colossae, founded by one of Paul's assistants. Christians met in the large hall of his house for worship and fellowship. Paul's letter would have been read to them there. The fact that it was treasured, and handed down to become part of our New Testament, shows that there had been

STONE WATER CONDUIT AT LAODICEA

a happy ending to the story of the runaway slave. This beautiful letter is the only one in our New Testament sent to an individual rather than to a church.

Colossae was an important town on the trade route between Ephesus and the valley of the river Euphrates. Laodicea, ten miles to the west, also lay on the trade route between east and west. It was a prosperous town whose bankers were known throughout the empire. The church at Laodicea was one of the seven churches to which the later Book of Revelation was addressed. The writer of Revelation condemned the church at Laodicea for being "luke-warm"—neither hot nor cold—in its faith (Revelation 3. 14-15). He may have been making a parable from daily life at Laodicea. In the ruins of the town can still be seen the remains of its theatres, its stadium and gymnasium and city gate, and of the terra-cotta pipes which brought water to the town. The water may have been brought by aqueduct from the hot springs of Hierapolis. In that case the water would be "luke-warm", just like the Christians of the town.

Hierapolis, six miles from Colossae, was famous for its guilds of rich dyers. Its hot springs were sacred to pagan nature religions, and they made the town a centre of healing. Huge baths, a gymnasium, and two theatres, found in the ruins, show what a large and wealthy city it must have been. The larger theatre, built during Roman times, was 325 feet wide at the front and the tiers of stone seats are still as they were in the time of Paul.

THE THEATRE AT HIERAPOLIS,
a reconstruction of some of the seats

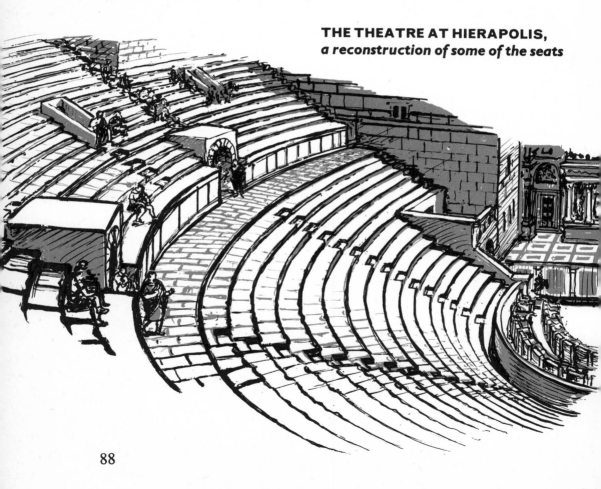

These three churches of the Lycus valley show the way in which Paul's strategy successfully spread the Gospel from a key city to the neighbouring towns. His ministry at Ephesus had made it a great centre of Christian missionary work. The church at Ephesus became the leading church of all the churches of Asia Minor. Among the great names connected with it were John the apostle and his disciple, John the elder, from whom came the Fourth Gospel. The New Testament also contains a letter of Paul called the *"Letter to the Ephesians"*. It was written later, when Paul was a prisoner at Rome, if it was written by Paul himself. Some scholars think that it was written by one of his disciples. It seems to have been a circular letter to all the churches in the Roman province of Asia.

Churches in Greece

After leaving Ephesus, Paul went northwards along the coast to the port of Troas. He had many worries. It seems, from his letters, that there had been trouble with the Jews at Ephesus and that Paul may even have been imprisoned there. It was certainly Jews from Ephesus who were later to raise the riot against Paul at Jerusalem which started his long imprisonment. There were troubles, too, at Corinth, and Paul had sent Titus on to deal with them. Gentile members of the church at Corinth were falling back into their pagan ways. They were even abusing the fellowship meal, with its commemoration of the Last Supper. There were divisions and rivalries between the Paul party and the Apollos party. Paul himself was very ill and hampered by his physical weakness.

Paul sailed once more from Troas to Europe to revisit his

churches. He must have gone to Philippi, to Thessalonica and to Berea. But he was eager to get to Corinth to deal with the grave problems in the church there. He spent three months of winter at Corinth and it was during this time that he wrote his greatest letter of all—the "*Epistle to the Romans*". There was already a church at Rome which Paul longed to visit. His plan was to visit Rome on his way to Spain.

But his immediate plan was to visit Jerusalem. He and his assistants were making a collection among the churches to take to the church of Jerusalem. Christians there deliberately chose to live in poverty, and they depended on the gifts of their brothers. The collection from all the Gentile churches would be a fine expression of the brotherhood of all Christians.

Paul planned to reach Jerusalem in time to keep the Feast of Pentecost there. He intended to travel from Corinth by a ship taking Jewish pilgrims to Jerusalem for the Feast. But plots against Paul came to light. The Jews planned to get rid of him during the voyage, which they could easily have done. Paul therefore began the return journey by land. He returned through Macedonia to Philippi, where Luke joined his party. Some went on ahead to Troas. Paul remained at Philippi for the Passover before sailing with Luke for Troas, reaching the port in five days.

Paul at Troas

It was quite a large party that gathered at Troas. The missionaries came from different towns, showing how the Church had spread through Paul's work. They came from both Greece and Asia Minor. Luke's list reads:

Sopater	—	Berea
Aristarchus	—	Thessalonica
Luke	—	Philippi
Gaius	—	Derbe
Timothy	—	Lystra
Tychicus, Trophimus	—	Ephesus

All were carrying collections from the churches of Asia Minor and Greece for the church at Jerusalem.

The whole party stayed at Troas for a week, perhaps waiting for a suitable ship. Luke tells of a typical Christian service there. It was held on the first day of the week, our Sunday, the day of Christ's rising from the dead—not on the Jewish sabbath, our Saturday. The day began at nightfall, about 6 p.m., on the evening before, as did the Jewish sabbath. First there was the "love-feast", the common meal of fellowship, then an address by the apostle, then the breaking of bread in commemoration of the Last Supper. The Christian meeting-place was the upper room of one of the tall blocks of houses that were built in Roman times.

A ROMAN HOUSE

This house, in the Forum of Trajan at Rome, shows the typically tall Roman house, with its large windows. The young man at Troas may have been sitting in such a window.

The meeting went on into the early hours of the morning, in the crowded upper room on the third storey, lit by many flickering, smoky lamps. Luke tells how one young man, perched on a window-sill, slipped and fell down on to the pavement of the inner court-yard. He recovered, under Paul's care, and the assembly went on to the breaking of bread. It was daylight before the meeting broke up.

Paul at Miletus
The party took a ship from Troas. It was a small coastal vessel, hugging the land and dropping anchor each night because of the tricky channels between the mainland and the islands dotted off the coast. Paul himself decided to walk on the 20 miles to the port of Assos, joining the ship there. Sailing 30 miles further south, the ship dropped anchor at Mitylene, chief city of the island of Lesbos and famous as the home of Sappho, the Greek poetess. Other night anchorages were off the island of Chios, said to have been the birthplace of Homer; Samos, a trading centre; and Trogyllium, a promontory just south of Ephesus. The next day brought the ship to Miletus.

The port of Miletus lay 36 miles south of Ephesus. Here Paul's ship was held up for two days. He seized the opportunity to make contact with the elders of the church of Ephesus. They came readily overland to Miletus when they received Paul's message. He talked with them, while his ship was making the final preparations for sailing, at the harbour of Miletus. The ancient port had been rebuilt, after its capture by Alexander the Great, as a typical Greek city. It had the customary AGORA, or market-place, surrounded by shops and public buildings. Like Corinth and Athens,

B l a c k   S e a

ASIA

Troas
Assos
Lesbos
Mitylene
Chios
Samos
•EPHESUS
•Miletus
Cos
Rhodes
CRETE

Patara

Taurus Mountains

)(Cilician Gates

•Tarsus

•ANTIOCH

CYPRUS

Tyre
Ptolemais
Caesarea
•JERUSALEM

Mediterranean Sea

PAUL'S VOYAGE
BACK TO PALESTINE

miles

0   150

above 1200 feet

it had a fine long street leading from the town to the harbour. Its large ruins include temples dedicated to Apollo and Athene. Archaeologists found at Miletus the largest open-air theatre in Asia Minor. On one of the blocks of seats was the Greek inscription—PLACE OF THE JEWS, ALSO CALLED GOD-FEARERS.

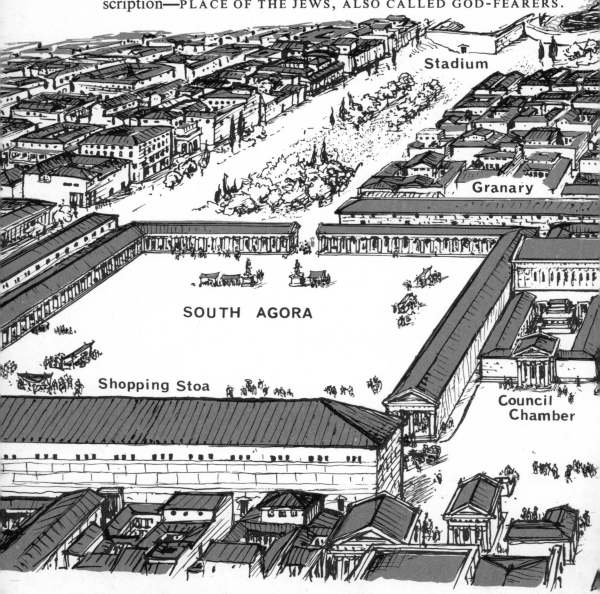

MILETUS HARBOUR

Theatre

North Agora

Lion Harbour

Gymnasium

Delphinium
(sacred to Apollo)

Paul's address to the elders at Miletus is one of the most moving passages in the New Testament. Luke records it just as he had heard it. Paul reminded the elders of how he had lived and worked among them, showing them his hands, rough and hardened from tent-making. He had faithfully ministered to them, preaching only the Gospel of Jesus. Now he was on his way to Jerusalem, knowing full well the dangers that awaited him there. Everywhere hostile Jews had attacked and maligned him. Everywhere prophets had foretold only suffering for him at Jerusalem. But his life mattered nothing to him compared with faithfully fulfilling his ministry to the very end. They would not see him again. They must remain faithful, too, as shepherds of the flock of Jesus.

The meeting ended with prayer as they kneeled down together by the harbour. There were tearful embraces as the elders bade farewell to Paul. Then he went on board, and the ship weighed anchor and bore him away.

Paul's voyage to Tyre

The coastal ship's next anchorage was at the island of Cos, famous as a centre of healing. It had a shrine to Asklepios, the Greek god of healing. It was the home of the Greek healer, Hippocrates, still famous today as the "father of medicine" and the author of the "Hippocratic Oath". The medical school at Cos, and the ointments it produced, contributed to the prosperity of the island.

The last stop was at Rhodes, the "island of roses", famous for its wines which were exported in special jars throughout the Mediterranean world. The jar handles, stamped with the maker's name and the date, have been found everywhere, thousands in Palestine. They help archaeologists in fixing dates and the size of towns, in their excavations. Rhodes was a great trading centre for ships crossing the Mediterranean Sea between Greece and Syria and between Egypt and the Black Sea. The fine coins of Rhodes, stamped with its rose symbol and the image of the sun-god Apollo, have been found in many lands. They show how widespread was the island's trade.

As ships entered the main harbour of Rhodes they passed its famous Colossus, one of the Seven Wonders of the ancient world. The bronze statue, 105 feet high, was a figure of the sun-god Apollo, set up in 280 B.C. to commemorate the island's deliverance from a siege. But an earthquake destroyed the Colossus in 224 B.C. Its remains had been lying in the harbour for nearly three centuries when Paul's ship lay at anchor. Centuries later, the Christian

THE COLOSSUS OF RHODES

Crusaders of the Middle Ages built a walled city here, and also a Gate in honour of St. Paul above the harbour.

The coastal sailing ship ended its trip, next day, at the port of Patara, east of Rhodes, famed for its shrine of Apollo. There Paul and his party changed ship. They boarded a much bigger vessel for the voyage to Palestine. It sailed across open sea, skirting the island of Cyprus, making direct for Tyre, the famous seaport of Phoenicia.

Paul in Palestine

Throughout Old Testament times Tyre had been a great commercial centre of the sea-going Phoenician traders. Its people had no ambitions on land, and they seldom became involved with wars. But their city's fine strategic position and its great wealth were always tempting to conquerors. Tyre was famous for its purple dyes, its glassware and its metal-work, rare and precious products. Its people thought themselves safe in their island city off the shore. But in 332 B.C. Alexander the Great had conquered it, after a long siege, by building a causeway from the mainland, nearly a quarter of a mile long. Tyre was rebuilt after his destruction. Though it was never again an independent city, it remained an important trading centre in the time of Paul.

Paul's large sea-going ship needed a week at Tyre to unload its cargo and to take on its new cargo and stores. There was a group of Christians at Tyre, though none of the party knew them. Yet, once they had met, there was a true sense of brotherhood between the missionaries and the church at Tyre. Luke records the touching detail that the Tyrian Christians brought their wives and children with them to the shore when the time came to say goodbye.

98

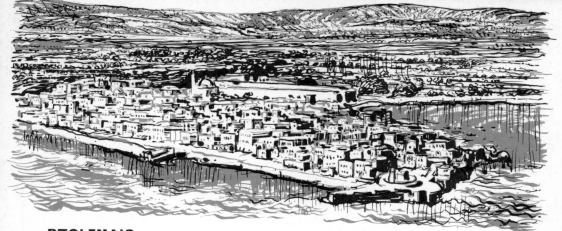

PTOLEMAIS

The voyage ended at Ptolemais, 25 miles south of Tyre. In Old Testament times its name was ACCHO ("Curve") and this survives in its modern name of Acre. The curving bay was the entrance to the ·Plain of Esdraelon. Paul and his party came ashore and went on by land to Caesarea, 30 miles to the south.

Paul at Caesarea

Caesarea was a fine Roman city, built by Herod the Great, and named in honour of the emperor Augustus. Skilled engineers had made an artificial harbour, 120 feet deep, with a great stone mole and breakwater. It was the Roman port of Palestine. The Romans also made Caesarea the official residence of the Governor of Judaea, and thus the capital of the land.

The fine city buildings included a temple in honour of Augustus, a theatre for Greek plays and musical performances, a stadium, and an open Forum surrounded by shops. The amphitheatre of Caesarea enclosed an oval larger than the Colosseum at Rome— 500 feet long and 200 feet wide. Here gladiators fought with wild beasts, just as they did at Rome.

*Caesarea harbour shown on
a coin, 6 B.C. - 4 A.D.*

100

a reconstruction

Caesarea was a pagan city to Jews. Here was lit the first flame of open Jewish revolt against the Romans. It led to four years of bitter war and ended in the destruction of Jerusalem in A.D. 70. Here there had been a Christian church from almost the beginning of the new faith. Peter had first preached to Gentiles here and had baptized the household of Cornelius, an officer of the Roman troops stationed at Caesarea. Philip, one of the seven deacons, had settled at Caesarea. He is known, now, as Philip the "Evangelist" or "preacher of the Good News". Apostles, Evangelists, and inspired Prophets were the three kinds of ministers in these early years of the Church.

Paul and his party were warmly welcomed into the home of Philip and his four daughters. They stayed for some days at Caesarea. Luke would have heard from Philip himself the stories of Philip's earlier missionary travels that are recorded in the earlier chapters of Luke's history (Acts 8. 4-8 and 26-39).

During Paul's stay at Caesarea there came a prophet from Jerusalem, named Agabus. He foretold suffering for Paul at Jerusalem, as so many others had done, at the hands of his bitter Jewish enemies. Everyone tried to deter Paul from going to Jerusalem, but again he insisted that he was ready to die for his faith in Jesus. Agabus had acted his prophecy by wrapping Paul's girdle around his hands and feet. Luke had already told in his Gospel how Jesus had set his face to go to Jerusalem, determined to face his enemies, ready to suffer and die. Now he was telling of the coming passion of Paul who, like his Master, set his face to go to Jerusalem.

It was an overland journey of 64 miles to Jerusalem. The heat

102

made it quite impossible to complete the journey in one day. There were, in any case, two days before the Feast of Pentecost which Paul was determined to keep at Jerusalem. The party saddled their donkeys and pack-mules, bearing the collection for the Jerusalem church. A Christian from Cyprus, named Mnason, set off with them, for they were to break their journey at his home for the night *en route*. So, on the following day, Paul came to Jerusalem.

To find and read in your Bible

To map

Make your own map of the third missionary journey of Paul, adding to it the places mentioned in this chapter.

To design

Design a letter-card for the city of Ephesus, which visitors to the city might buy to post back to their friends at home. It will be made up of pictures of the main "sights" of the city. You can draw or paint your pictures.

To act

Act the scene when Demetrius the silversmith called a meeting of his fellow-craftsmen. Different speakers will bring up the various arguments why Paul must be attacked, and suggest how this can be done.

To report
Imagine that you were a newspaper reporter at Ephesus. Write up a report for your readers of the "Riot at Ephesus", telling them what caused the riot and what happened during it.

To research
You have read in this chapter of two of the "Seven Wonders" of the ancient world, and of some of the others in previous books in this series. Use reference books to find out all you can about these Seven Wonders. Draw each of them, with the story and description of each one.

To imagine

Imagine that you were Onesimus, the runaway slave. Write or tell the story of what happened to you from when you ran away until you came back to your master, Philemon, with Paul's letter. Some of the details of your story can be imaginary. Read the Letter to Philemon, in a modern translation of the Bible, before you make up your story.

To design

Design some Greek coins, perhaps for some of the places visited by Paul. They will include images of the various gods, and symbols like the rose of Rhodes. Design also some Christian coins, using Christian symbols and images that you think would be fitting. Explain the various designs you have made.

To imagine

Imagine, if you are a girl, that you were one of the daughters of Philip the Evangelist, living at Caesarea. Describe your city, and tell what happened when Paul and his friends came to stay. If you are a boy, tell the same story as if you were a son of one of Philip's friends in the church at Caesarea - for example, Mnason.

To letter and learn

Write out, in illuminated lettering if you can, the saying of Jesus told by Paul to the elders at Miletus (Acts 20. 35). It is a fine saying to remember always.

A conversation to make up

A group of you can take the parts of Paul's assistants whom Luke lists, with their homes, in Acts 20. 4. Make up a conversation among yourselves about Paul, relating how you became Christians when he visited your homes, where you have been with him, what you have done for him, and telling of your fears for his coming visit to Jerusalem.

To record and remember
Write out the famous "Hymn of Love", written by Paul in a letter during this missionary journey (1 Corinthians 13. 1-13). Write it from a modern translation of the Bible. Learn verses 4-7 by heart.

To draw
Make up a strip-cartoon of your own drawings, picturing some of the main events that happened on this third missionary journey of Paul.

A large Phoenician merchant ship, with sails hoisted
From a tomb found at Sidon

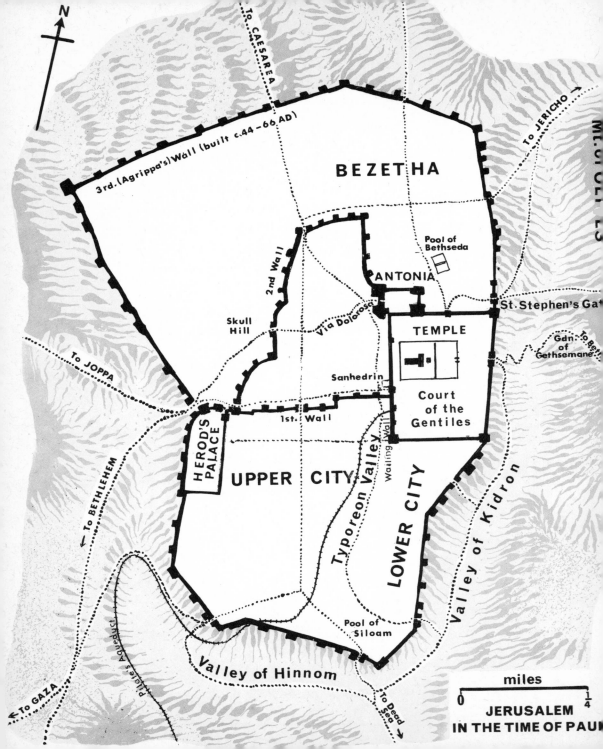

JERUSALEM IN THE TIME OF PAUL

Paul A Prisoner

Paul at Jerusalem

Paul and his party received a warm welcome from the Christian Jews of Jerusalem. This was an informal greeting. But the following day there was an official meeting with the leaders of the church. James, the brother of Jesus, was head of the Jerusalem church, assisted by elders. None of the apostles are mentioned. They must all have left Jerusalem, by now, on missionary journeys.

At this meeting, Paul would have formally handed over the collection made by the churches of Greece and Asia Minor for the Jerusalem church. It was to be a symbol of the brotherhood between all Christians, both Jews and Gentiles. It would prove Paul's loyalty and goodwill to the Jewish church of Jerusalem, and help towards unity and understanding. But Luke does not mention the collection, for it had failed in its purpose.

This official meeting was not a happy one. James and the elders may have had friendly feelings for Paul, but they were in an awkward position. They were only left in peace by their fellow-Jews because they kept up all the practices of their Jewish religion. But they were not popular. Some years before, they had been persecuted by Herod Agrippa I, grandson of Herod the Great. He had been brought up at Rome where he had become a favourite of the emperor Caligula. He had been given territory to rule over, and it had been increased by the next emperor, Claudius. From A.D. 41-44 Herod Agrippa had ruled over almost as large a kingdom as that of Herod the Great. He was an enthusiast for Greek culture. But he publicly supported the religion of the Jews in order to win their favour. For the same reason he persecuted the Christian Jews of Jerusalem. It was he who had put to death the apostle James, among others, and who had imprisoned Peter. On the death of Herod Agrippa, shortly after, the Romans replaced him by Procurators. Under them the church at Jerusalem was left in peace. But Jewish hostility might break out again at any time. James and the elders must therefore do nothing that might offend the Jews. They knew well that Paul was hated by many Jews as a traitor to their race and to their religion. His presence among them was embarrassing. Somehow he must prove his loyalty to Jewish religion, if they were to be left in peace.

The meeting began with Paul giving an account of his work abroad. The leaders of the Jerusalem church gave thanks to God for his blessing of this work among Gentiles. But they immediately went on to raise the urgent problem before them. Many Jews were members of these Gentile churches. Rumours from all sides said that Paul had taught these Christian Jews not to bother any more about the sacred Jewish Law. The Council of Jerusalem had certainly agreed that Gentiles need not accept the Jewish Law in order to enter the Christian Church. But it had not said that Jews could abandon the Law. Something must be done quickly. Jerusalem was packed with Jewish pilgrims from abroad. Paul would soon be recognised by his enemies. He must show publicly that he was a loyal Jew, and so disprove the rumours. That was the only way in which he, and all Christian Jews at Jerusalem, would be safe from attack.

Paul agreed to carry out the proposal which James made. There

110

were four poor Jews in the church who had taken vows as NAZI-RITES or DEDICATED ONES. Such vows were very ancient among the Jews. They were taken by pious men who showed their religious devotion by strict self-denial. They were looked up to, and it was a custom for other Jews to pay the necessary fees to the temple for such dedicated men. Herod Agrippa I had paid for many Nazirites to take their vows when he had been made king. By this outward act of piety he sought to win popularity with the Jews. Paul could do this, too. He could go to the temple with the four poor Jews, pay their offerings, share their vows, and prove his loyalty to Jewish religion—to both Law and temple.

The temple at Jerusalem

Paul duly went to the temple with the four Nazirites. It took seven days for all of them to complete their vows. Paul may not have intended to stay so long at Jerusalem. The days were almost ended when the crisis came. Paul was recognised by some Jewish pilgrims from Asia, probably from Ephesus. They had seen Paul, some days before, with a Gentile from Ephesus named Trophimus. He had become a Christian and had been Paul's assistant in his work in Asia. Now he had come to Jerusalem with Paul's party, bringing the collection from the churches of Asia. These hostile Jews of Ephesus had seen Paul with Trophimus in the outer court where Gentiles were allowed. Now, seeing Paul in the inner court where Gentiles were strictly forbidden, they cried out that Paul had desecrated the temple.

In ancient times, most temples were divided up into different parts, with strict rules of admission to each one according to its

111

sacredness. The temple at Jerusalem was like this. All around it lay an esplanade, an outer court, called THE COURT OF THE GENTILES. Men of any race could walk here. A low barrier separated this outer court from the INNER TEMPLE. Around this barrier, or "wall of partition", were notices warning Gentiles that if they went any further they would be liable to death. The notices were written in Hebrew and Greek and Latin so that no Gentile could fail to understand the grave and solemn warning. One of the Greek inscriptions was found in 1871 in a cemetery. It runs:

> LET NO ONE OF THE GENTILES ENTER INSIDE THE BAR-RIER AROUND THIS SANCTUARY AND THE PORCH. AND IF HE TRANSGRESSES HE SHALL HIMSELF BEAR THE BLAME FOR HIS SUBSEQUENT DEATH.

The Romans had agreed to the death penalty for such an offence, knowing that it would lead to a riot. Nothing provoked the Jews more than any offence against their religion, as a number of Roman administrators had learnt to their cost, among them Pontius Pilate.

The Inner Temple had two courts. The outer one was called THE COURT OF THE WOMEN. Jewish women could enter here, but they could go no further. Only Jewish males were allowed into the INNER COURT. In one corner of it was the "House of the Nazirites". It was here that the Jews from Ephesus saw Paul making his vows with the four poor Jews whom he had agreed to sponsor. It was in this Inner Court that the temple building stood, with the altar before it. Only priests could enter the temple itself. Only the high priest might enter its most sacred part, THE HOLY OF HOLIES, and then only on one day in the year, the sacred Day of Atonement.

112

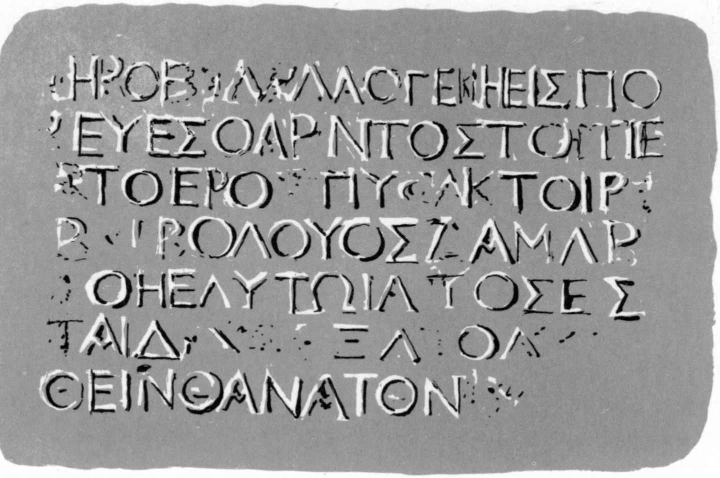

ΗΡΟΒ·ΛΚΛΛΟΓΕΝΗΕΙΣΠΟ
ΕΥΕΣΟΑΡ·ΝΤΟΣΤΟΠΕ
ΡΤΟΕΡΟ·ΠΥΣΑΚΤΟΙΡ·
Β·ΙΡΟΛΟΥΟΣΖΑΜΛΡ
ΟΗΕΛΥΤΩΙΑΤΟΣΕ·Σ
ΤΑΙΔ·ΞΛΙΟΛ
ΘΕΙΝΘΑΝΑΤΟΝ

**THE WARNING INSCRIPTION TO GENTILES
BETWEEN THE OUTER COURT AND INNER COURT
OF THE TEMPLE**

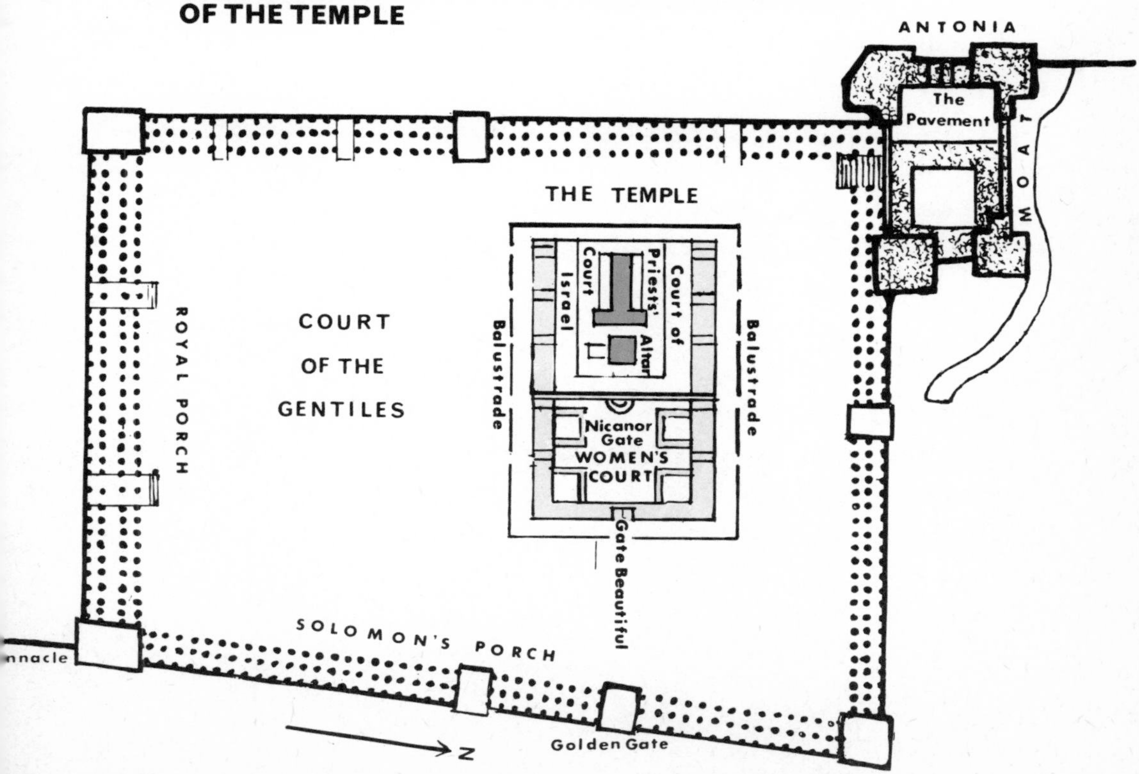

ANTONIA

The Pavement

M O A T

THE TEMPLE

Court of Priests'
Israel Court
Altar

Nicanor
Gate
WOMEN'S
COURT

ROYAL PORCH

COURT
OF THE
GENTILES

Balustrade

Balustrade

Gate Beautiful

SOLOMON'S PORCH

Pinnacle

N

Golden Gate

The temple courts were thronged with pilgrims from all over the world, gathered for the Feast of Pentecost. Once the Jews from Ephesus had raised their cry against Paul, tumult quickly broke out. They charged Paul with the worst crimes of all—being a traitor to his people, speaking against the Law, blaspheming against the house of God by bringing a Gentile into the sacred inner court. In the electric atmosphere the riot quickly grew. Paul was seized and dragged out through the temple courts to be stoned to death.

The Roman garrison
Paul was only saved from a violent death at the hands of the mob by the Roman garrison at the temple. A flight of stone steps led down from their headquarters, the FORTRESS OF ANTONIA, directly on to the outer court of the temple area. Here they were at hand, especially during the turbulent feasts, for just such a riot as this.

The Fortress of Antonia was at the north-west corner of the temple. There had been two strong towers, in this area, far back in the days of King David and his son Solomon. They were replaced, in the time of Nehemiah, by a fortress which was given the Persian name, "Baris". The Maccabean leaders had made the Baris into a royal palace. Herod the Great had moved to another royal residence. He had made the Baris into a strong Fortress and renamed it as "Fortress of Antonia" in honour of Mark Antony, the Roman leader who ruled the east in his time. The Fortress had four lofty towers, different in shape, surrounding an inner courtyard where some think Jesus may have stood before Pilate. The massive walls of the Fortress made it an ideal headquarters for the Roman garrison of Jerusalem. From its high towers, overlooking the whole temple area, guards could spot any disorder instantly and troops be sent to deal with it.

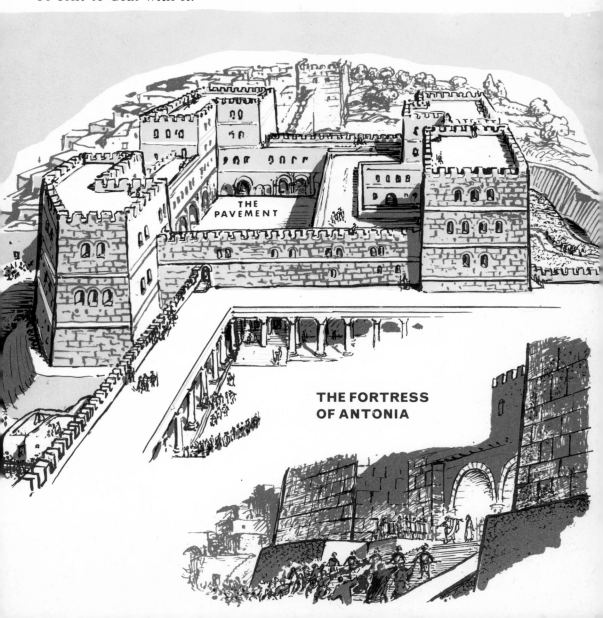

THE PAVEMENT

THE FORTRESS OF ANTONIA

As soon as the riot was reported, the garrison commander hurried down into the temple court with a band of officers and men. His name was Claudius Lysias. His rank was that of "chiliarch"—commander of a cohort. A cohort was made up of a maximum of 600 men, with some supporting cavalry, ten such cohorts making up a legion. Luke records that the commander had Paul bound with two chains and demanded to know the charges made against him. He could learn nothing in the general uproar. He ordered Paul to be taken into the castle, but even the troops had difficulty in getting him there safely through the enraged mob. Luke watched as the soldiers lifted Paul up and passed him over their heads up the stairway to the Fortress.

When Paul reached safety at the top of the steps he asked the commander if he might speak. Claudius Lysias was astonished at Paul's fluent Greek, showing him to be a cultured man. He had jumped to other conclusions about Paul's identity. He was well aware that there was an underground movement of Jewish patriots called ZEALOTS. They believed in resisting the Romans by force and they planned for open revolt against their oppressors. One of them, Simon the Zealot, had become an apostle of Jesus. The most fanatic of the Zealots were assassins called "sicarii" from the "sicae", short daggers, which they secretly carried. They murdered any Jews whom they thought to be too friendly with the Romans. There had been several open revolts against Rome. The latest had been led by an Egyptian, with 4,000 sicarii under him. He had gathered this rabble on the Mount of Olives. He proclaimed that, at his command, the walls of the city would fall, just as the walls of Jericho had fallen at Joshua's command. Then his followers could plunder the city and take patriotic revenge on the Romans and their Jewish friends. Roman troops had soon dealt with the deluded followers of the Egyptian, but their leader had escaped. Claudius Lysias had jumped to the conclusion that Paul was the Egyptian, now recognised by the survivors of his disillusioned followers. That would explain their savage attack upon Paul and their attempt to murder him.

THE PAVEMENT OF THE COURTYARD IN THE FORTRESS OF ANTONIA

This pavement lies today beneath a convent school. It is about 165 feet square, and it is made of thick lime-stone blocks each 3 feet square. On it can still be seen the scratchings made by Roman soldiers for their gambling games. This may be the 'Pavement' where Jesus stood before Pilate (John 19.13). But some scholars think that the Procurator's residence in Jerusalem was not the Fortress of Antonia but Herod's Palace, and that the 'Pavement' was the open space in front of it. This would explain the presence of a crowd of Jews, for the Romans would not have opened the Fortress of Antonia to them.

117

Paul and the garrison commander

Paul quickly answered the Roman's accusation that he was the Egyptian fanatic. "I am a Jew of Tarsus", he replied, "a citizen of no mean city". Any educated man would recognise this reference to the famous Greek poet, Euripides. Paul was clearly a man of culture, despite his appearance. The commander readily agreed when Paul asked if he might speak to the crowd of Jews at the foot of the steps, held at bay by the Roman guards. Claudius Lysias was not trying to please Paul. As commander of the garrison, he was responsible for law and order in the city during the Governor's absence. He had to hear legal cases, and give decisions, as a magistrate. He was, in fact, a "tribune" or "military governor". He had to get this riot over as soon as possible. Paul was clearly no ruffian. He might quieten the crowd and disperse them.

Paul stretched out his arm, as the custom was for public speakers in Roman times—for bodily gestures played an important part in oratory. He spoke in Aramaic, the language of the Jews, and that brought the crowd to silence. Many of them could not have known, in any case, whom Paul was and what exactly he had done. Paul spoke of his strict upbringing in the Jewish Law, of his study under the great rabbi Gamaliel, of his loyal persecution of the

Christian sect, of his willing presence at the stoning of Stephen. It was a divine revelation on the road to Damascus that had changed his life. It was a vision in the temple itself that had bidden him preach to Gentiles. Paul got no further than the mention of the hated word "Gentiles". The crowd broke into an uproar once again, shrieking for his death.

The Roman commander had learned nothing from Paul's words. And, far from quieting the crowd, Paul had driven them into a frenzy. He must examine Paul himself in the security of the Fortress. There he ordered Paul to be bound for flogging. It was a Roman custom to scourge accused men before questioning so as to get full confession. As the soldiers were binding him with thongs, Paul said to the ·centurion standing by—"You realise that it is illegal to flog a man who is a Roman Citizen, and whose case has not even been heard?" The centurion reported at once to the tribune and he came hurrying out. It was against Roman law to punish a man before he had even been heard, let alone condemned. It was a crime of the worst order to punish a Roman Citizen. The tribune would be guilty on both counts if what Paul said was true.

Paul repeated to the tribune that he was a Roman Citizen. "I paid a great deal of money for my Citizenship", the tribune said, accusingly. His very name proved that. Lysias was a Greek name. "Claudius" had been added to it to show that he had bought his citizenship during the reign of the emperor Claudius—a time when the sale of such honours had been very common. Paul answered with simple pride, "I was born a Roman Citizen." At once the tribune ordered him to be freed from his bonds. He had done more than enough in even binding a Roman Citizen.

119

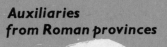
Auxiliaries from Roman provinces

ROMAN SOLDIERS

Baggage train

Legionaries and standards

Chiliarch ("colonel")

Centurion

Standard bearer

Camp made on
the march

Legionary

Auxiliary
from Gaul

Archers

Siege equipment

Legionary cavalry

Vanguard

Roadmakers and
camp constructors

General
and his staff

Paul before the Jewish Council

Claudius Lysias had still to discover what exactly the charges were against Paul. He called a meeting of the Sanhedrin, the Council of the Jews, for the following day. This was a reasonable thing to do. The Council was recognised by the Romans as the representative body for the Jewish people, with power to order their affairs. To bring Paul before the Council would help him in giving judgement on his case. Besides, it would please the Jews and keep them from any more rioting.

Paul was brought before the Council under a strong guard. Luke, it seems, was not at the meeting and he only gives a short account of it. Charges must have been made against Paul, and there had been some debate before Paul made his defence. He began by professing that his conscience was clear before God. At this, the high priest Ananias ordered that Paul should be struck on the face. Paul responded by calling him, in the proverbial saying, "a whitened wall". It came from the Jewish custom of white-washing tombs so that everyone could avoid them. Nothing was more defiling, in Jewish religion, than having any contact with the dead. Paul meant that the high priest, outwardly an upholder of the Law, was breaking it by having him struck.

A JEWISH TOMB
This tomb of a rabbi at Tiberias illustrates the Jewish proverbial saying - 'a whitened wall'.

The Council was mainly made up of Sadducees and Pharisees, who had many differences between them. The Sadducees lived by the ancient written Law. They were made up of the aristocratic priestly families of Jerusalem. The Pharisees were a party of devout laymen. They added their own unwritten traditions to the Law, seeking to make it apply to every part of daily life. They had developed other beliefs, too, which the Sadducees also rejected. They included belief in angels, in resurrection from the dead, and in the coming of the Messiah.

Paul now cried out that he was a Pharisee, and that the charge against him arose from his belief in angels and in resurrection and in the Messiah. At once the Council broke into an uproar as Pharisees and Sadduceees argued fiercely with each other. This was not just a trick on Paul's part. As a Pharisee, he had been brought up to believe in the Messiah, in angels, and in resurrection. He had simply applied these beliefs to his new faith in Jesus, who fulfilled them. Pharisees agreed with these beliefs, even though they thought Paul to be wrong in applying them to Jesus. Sadducees rejected these beliefs, as well as Jesus. The Pharisees in the Council were on Paul's side. They accepted angelic visions, such as Paul had claimed. It would be fighting against God to condemn Paul. They declared him innocent. Tumult broke out, worse than ever, between the Pharisees and Sadducees in the Council.

Claudius Lysias was still none the wiser. It seemed that the whole affair was a domestic dispute among Jews about their religion. He could still find nothing criminal in Paul, and he had to protect him as a Roman Citizen. It was obvious that Paul would be pulled to pieces if he were not protected. The tribune had him

escorted back by strong guard to the Fortress of Antonia.

That night, Paul had another vision. It seemed that Jesus stood by him, telling Paul that he must preach the Gospel at Rome. His experience gave Paul new strength and hope for the future.

Paul at Caesarea

It is now that Paul's own family come, for the first time, into Luke's history. His sister had married into an important family at Jerusalem, perhaps one of the priestly families of the Sadducees. Her son discovered a plot against his uncle, Paul. Forty Jews had vowed to fast until they had killed him. They could not get near Paul while he was in the safety of the Fortress. They asked the leaders of the Council to request that Paul be brought before them the following day for further questioning of his beliefs. This would seem quite reasonable to the tribune. The conspirators would lie in wait for Paul.

The boy came to the Fortress to tell Paul of the plot against him.

124

PAUL BEFORE THE SANHEDRIN

Paul sent him to the tribune who bade the boy tell no one that he had revealed the plot. Then he laid his plans. He had to act quickly and decisively to protect himself, as well as Paul. He was not only afraid that a Roman Citizen might be killed while in his care. One early manuscript adds that he had another fear. The Jews, after killing Paul, could put round the story that the tribune had accepted a bribe to let them do it. A former Governor of the Jews, Cumanus by name, had been accused of similar bribery. He had been punished with banishment. Thus, the tribune had every reason to keep Paul safe. He must get him away from Jerusalem to the Governor's residence at Caesarea. There Paul would be out of his responsibility. The Governor himself could deal with this troublesome case.

The tribune ordered the strongest escort possible. It was made up of 200 foot soldiers, 70 horsemen, and 200 spearmen. The tribune was determined to leave nothing to chance. Paul travelled by mule, surrounded by nearly 500 armed men. They left at dead of night, taking the Roman military road to Caesarea. It ran by way of Bethhoron and Lydda to the town of Antipatris, 39 miles from Jerusalem. Antipatris, known as Aphek in Old Testament times, had been rebuilt by Herod the Great and renamed in honour of his father, Antipater. Here, more than halfway to Caesarea, there was no more danger from the Jews. After camping for the night, the foot soldiers were sent back to Jerusalem. Paul was taken on to Caesarea, escorted by the cavalry.

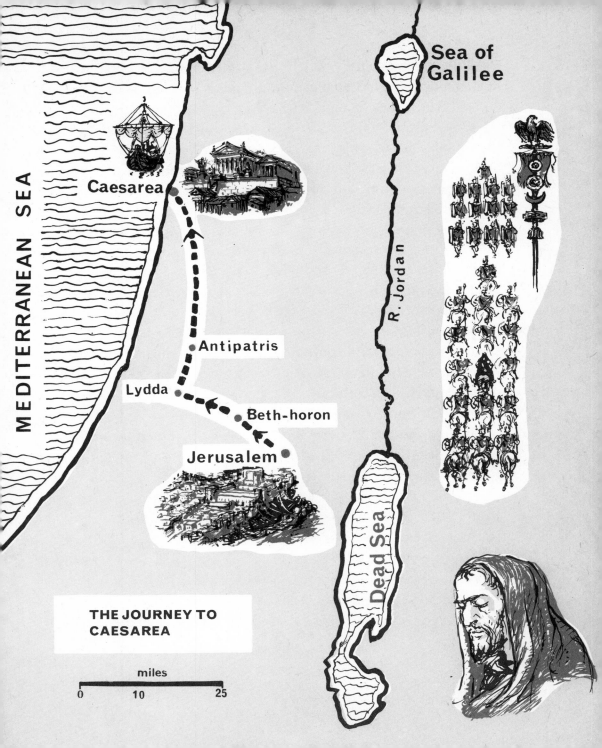

Sea of Galilee

MEDITERRANEAN SEA

Caesarea

R. Jordan

• **Antipatris**

Lydda •

• **Beth-horon**

Jerusalem •

Dead Sea

**THE JOURNEY TO
CAESAREA**

miles

0   10   25

Paul before Felix

Antoninus Felix was at that time the Governor, or Procurator, of Judaea. He had won high office through his brother, a freedman who had become a favourite of the emperor Claudius. One Roman historian, Tacitus, says that Felix was well-known for his greed and cruelty. He was later to be recalled to Rome and tried for his cruelty in stamping out Jewish riots at Caesarea, and to be dismissed from his office.

Paul was brought before Felix on his arrival at Caesarea. The officer in charge presented the Governor with a letter from Claudius Lysias, the tribune at Jerusalem, describing Paul's case. Luke quotes it as if he is reproducing it. He may have heard it read out in court later. The tribune stated that he had found Paul to be innocent of any crime worthy of imprisonment or death. The case seemed to involve a dispute between Jews about their religion. In his letter the tribune made his own conduct of the matter to seem quite perfect. He certainly said nothing about having bound a Roman Citizen for punishment without trial.

The first concern of Felix was to make sure that Paul came under his authority. He was satisfied when he was told that Paul came from Cilicia, part of the Roman province of Syria. Felix was a deputy of the Legate who ruled the province. He could therefore hear Paul's case. But he postponed the hearing until Paul's accusers arrived from Jerusalem, five days later.

The delegation of Jews was led by the high priest, Ananias. They had hired a lawyer to present their case. His Roman name, Tertullus, and his skilful speech to the court show that he was a professional advocate. He began with flattering compliments to

A ROMAN ORATOR

The art of public speaking was highly developed among both Greeks and Romans. 'Rhetoric' was an important part of all education. A professional advocate like Tertullus would be a skilled orator. Paul was, too. We see this both in his speeches and in the gestures which he made, each of which had a meaning, and which were learnt as part of the art of public speaking.

Felix. Then he made three grave charges against Paul. First, he caused public disorder throughout the Roman empire. Secondly, he belonged to the Jewish sect of Nazarenes, followers of Jesus of Nazareth. This sect had been condemned by the Jewish leaders in their Council. It did not therefore share in the recognition given by Rome to the religion of the Jews. Thus the sect was illegal under Roman law. Thirdly, Paul had tried to profane the temple by bringing a Gentile into it; and this was a crime recognised by the Romans as punishable by death. All three charges were therefore crimes against Roman law.

The priests from Jerusalem warmly agreed with these charges, as presented by Tertullus. They had been cleverly twisted so as to make Paul into a Roman criminal rather than a Jewish heretic. Paul made his defence firmly and cheerfully, when Felix beckoned him to reply. He was confident, he said, because Felix knew the Jews and their religion so well. There was no proof whatever of the charges made against him. His twelve days in Jerusalem had been entirely spent in making vows in the temple. Far from profaning the temple, he had been showing his loyalty to Jewish religion. If he had committed an offence against the temple, why had the Jews from Ephesus not come to give evidence against him? The Council had found nothing against him, either. Paul admitted that he worshipped the God of the Jews in a different way from his opponents. The question at issue between them was belief in resurrection from the dead—and that was part of the beliefs of the Pharisees.

The hearing ended without a decision. The Governor's conclusion was AMPLIUS—the case needed further examination.

Paul and Felix

Felix was simply putting off making a decision. His excuse was that he must wait until the tribune at Jerusalem came down to Caesarea. Felix does not seem even to have sent for the tribune. He had several reasons for not reaching a decision. He was already in difficulties with the Jews and he had to consider them. He would keep Paul in custody in his Praetorium at Caesarea. This was his official residence as Governor, a combination of palace and fortress. It would please the Jews to have Paul imprisoned,

130

and there would be no further trouble while Paul was in custody. But Felix treated Paul well. He gave him into the care of a centurion. Paul was to be free to receive his friends and to do as he wished, provided that he did not leave the Praetorium.

Luke says that Felix was really waiting for a bribe from Paul. It seems that Paul must have come into money, and that Felix knew it. We have seen how, throughout his missionary journeys, Paul had worked at his craft of tent-making, so as not to be a burden to anyone. He may have done this deliberately, when there was no need, so as to help his work of spreading the Gospel. But now he had paid for the four poor Jews of Jerusalem to make their vows, and Felix would expect a very large bribe indeed. Whatever Paul's circumstances were, he would certainly not bribe his way out of prison.

TENT-MAKING

Paul wove goat's hair into a rough but very strong cloth. It was used for tents, sails, shoes, mats and all kinds of coverings. It made the skin of the tent-maker's hands grow black and coarse. Paul showed his hands to the elders at Miletus to prove how he had laboured, during his journeys, so as not to be a burden to anyone (Acts 20.33-35).

There was someone else whom Felix may have pleased by leaving Paul in custody. This was his third wife, Drusilla. She was the young and beautiful daughter of Herod Agrippa I, and granddaughter of Herod the Great. She was a Jewess, but she had broken the Jewish Law by deserting her husband to marry Felix. Their marriage was therefore evil to Jews. Some time later, Felix sent for Paul. He and his wife Drusilla wanted to hear about Paul's Christian religion. Luke says that Paul spoke to them of "righteousness, temperance, and judgement to come", and that Felix was afraid. He was a superstitious man and he had a bad conscience. Such a man would tremble when he heard of judgement in the life to come for his evil deeds.

Drusilla may well have been angered by Paul's words. He had certainly condemned her marriage with Felix, whether he had said it openly or not. It was like Herod and John the Baptist all over again. Herod had married his wife against the Law, too, and John the Baptist had openly condemned him. Herod's wife had got her revenge by having John imprisoned and finally put to death (Matthew 14. 3-12). Now Drusilla must have been wanting revenge, too. One early manuscript adds that Felix left Paul in custody to please his wife, Drusilla.

Felix

Drusilla

Two years at Caesarea

Felix sent for Paul several times. Luke says that he did this in the hope that Paul would offer him a large bribe in return for his freedom. Felix may also have found a certain thrill in Paul's fiery preaching.

Paul spent two years in the Praetorium at Caesarea. Luke tells us nothing about them. But we can be sure that Paul went on with his work as best he could, receiving messengers from his churches and sending his faithful assistants to them with messages and letters.

Luke himself was free to come and go. He would have spent much of his time with the church at Caesarea, especially with Philip the Evangelist. Philip could tell him much about the beginnings of the church at Jerusalem. During these two years, too, Luke would have collected memories of Jesus from many who had been with him during his earthly life. When he had gathered and sifted all the evidence, Luke wrote his Gospel. It contains 1,149 verses altogether. We know that some 320 of these verses were taken from Mark's Gospel, and about 250 verses from another source which was also used by the writer of Matthew's Gospel. That leaves over 400 verses, a third of Luke's Gospel, which we find nowhere else. These contain precious memories of Jesus and his teaching, among them the famous parables of the Good Samaritan and the Prodigal Son. These precious records of Jesus must have been gathered by Luke during those two years at Caesarea.

Festus the Governor

After two years, Felix was recalled to Rome to be tried, before the emperor Nero, for his cruelty against the Jews. He was replaced by Porcius Festus, a very different man. Festus was to die after only two years as Governor. Shortly after his death, there broke out the four years of bitter war between Jews and Romans that ended with the destruction of Jerusalem in A.D. 70. The evil and folly of the Roman Governors of Judaea were largely responsible for these cruel wars. Festus stood apart from the other Governors in his nobility of character. It was a tragedy that he was to die so soon.

Festus would have to clear up matters left unfinished by Felix, including the case of Paul. But the Jews had by no means forgotten Paul, and they quickly brought his case up before the new Governor. They must have hoped that they would get their way with him as a newcomer, unfamiliar with their people and their religion. Three days after arriving at Caesarea, Festus went up to Jerusalem. The leaders of the Council immediately asked for Paul to be brought before them at Jerusalem, so that the case could be decided. Festus was not to be meekly led by the leaders of the Jews. He decided that a Jewish delegation should return with him to Caesarea. He would open the case there.

Festus was a fine Roman administrator, firm and fair in giving justice. Neither popular passions, nor bribery, nor winning favour with the Jews swayed his judgement. But he was well aware of the difficulties of his post, and of his ignorance of Jewish ways. Clearly the case of Paul was a leading issue with the Jews and it had to be settled.

THE ROMAN EMPEROR NERO (A.D. 54-68)

Nero became emperor on the death of Claudius in A.D. 54. Felix was recalled and tried before Nero for his cruelty to the Jews. Nero appointed Festus in his place. Paul was sent to Rome to be tried before Nero. He was the first emperor to persecute Christians, blaming them for the fire of Rome in A.D. 64. Both Peter and Paul died during this persecution, according to ancient tradition.

135

Paul before Festus

On his return to Caesarea, Festus had Paul brought before him in the Judgement Hall. The Jews from Jerusalem were loud in their accusations against Paul. Paul stated simply but firmly that he was innocent of any offence against Jewish Law, the temple, or the Roman authorities. Festus asked Paul, as he was bound to do, whether he would be willing to have his case heard at Jerusalem, before the Council, the Governor himself presiding. This seemed perfectly fair and just to Festus. The Council of the Jews was recognised by the Romans as being responsible for running their internal affairs, and for administering their Law. Nothing could be fairer than to let the Jewish leaders thrash out the case, the Governor ensuring that strict justice was done.

To Paul, however, the matter was quite different. He had by now given up all hope of getting justice before the Jews. They cleverly twisted the charges, and they might even take in a fair-minded ruler like Festus. In any case, Festus was concerned most of all with law and order. Paul was clearly a storm centre among the Jews. It would not be easy for the Governor to release him, even if he were declared to be innocent.

It was now, therefore, that Paul made his famous decision. APPELLO CAESAREM—I APPEAL UNTO CAESAR, he said. It was the privilege of a Roman Citizen to have any case against him heard before the emperor himself at Rome. Once Paul claimed his privilege, his case was at once taken out of the hands of any other court. Festus briefly consulted his legal advisers, sitting with him. They were quite unanimous. Paul had appealed to Caesar— he must go to Caesar.

136

**PAUL IN THE JUDGEMENT HALL
OF THE PRAETORIUM AT CAESAREA**

Paul before Agrippa

It happened that, before Paul left for Rome, Festus had an important visitor. This was Herod Agrippa II, the seventh and last of the family of Herod the Great to bear rule in Palestine. He had been too young to succeed his father, Herod Agrippa I, as king of the Jews. By now he had become ruler over territory east of the river Jordan, opposite Galilee. As a practising Jew, familiar with Jewish religion, he had also been given charge of the temple at Jerusalem, with power to appoint the high priest. From his upbringing at Rome, he was also familiar with Roman ways and with Roman justice. The conscientious Festus thought that Agrippa would be the ideal person to hear the case of Paul.

FAMILY TREE OF THE HERODS

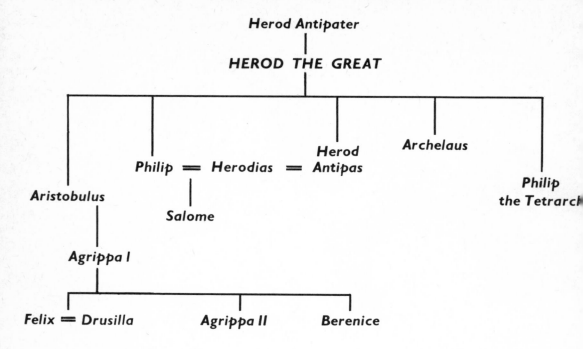

Agrippa came to Caesarea with his widowed sister, Berenice. She was as beautiful as her sister Drusilla, the illegal wife of the former Governor, Felix. Berenice was notorious for her evil life. After the fall of Jerusalem, in A.D. 70, she and Agrippa were to settle at Rome, living as Gentiles.

Paul's case had already been ended by his appeal to Rome. But Festus needed to send to Rome a full report on the case, and Agrippa could help him in deciding on the facts. Although Paul's hearing before Agrippa was not a trial, it was a great state occasion. Agrippa and Berenice entered the Judgement Hall in great pomp. The Hall was crowded with Roman officials and guards, as well

138

as with leading citizens of Caesarea. Festus began the hearing by saying publicly to Agrippa that, while the Jews clamoured for Paul's death, he had found him innocent of any crime. His case had now been transferred to Rome. But Festus would be grateful for Agrippa's opinion on the case to help him make his report.

Paul saw in this state occasion a wonderful opportunity to preach the Gospel. He had had plenty of time to prepare his speech, and this is shown in its precise Greek and in its careful arrangement. Paul spoke, as he had done before, of his strict Jewish upbringing and way of life; of the divine vision that had changed his life on the road to Damascus; of the resurrection that was part of the Jewish beliefs of the Pharisees; and of how the Old Testament had prophesied preaching to the Gentiles. The climax of his speech was that all the hopes of the Jewish prophets had been fulfilled in Jesus.

Coin of Herod Agrippa II

Bronze head of Berenice

139

The results of Paul's speech

Festus was astonished at all this. As a practical man of affairs, he would understand very little of it. But there was no doubting the fire that burned within Paul. Festus could only think that he must be possessed by a demon, a common belief in those days. Paul rejected any such idea. He turned towards Agrippa and demanded that the king should confirm that what he had said was reasonable. Agrippa knew the prophets' writings well. Did he not believe them? Agrippa turned aside Paul's demand with a jest. "You'll soon be thinking that you are making a Christian of me!" he joked. "I wish that you were, and all who hear me, too," Paul replied fervently.

Festus and his royal guests withdrew to talk among themselves. They soon agreed that Paul had done nothing to deserve imprisonment or death. Agrippa's opinion was quite definite. "If he had not appealed to Caesar, you could have set him free," he said to Festus. Once again, Luke was showing clearly that Roman officials found nothing illegal or criminal in the Christian faith.

Now all that remained was Paul's journey to Rome.

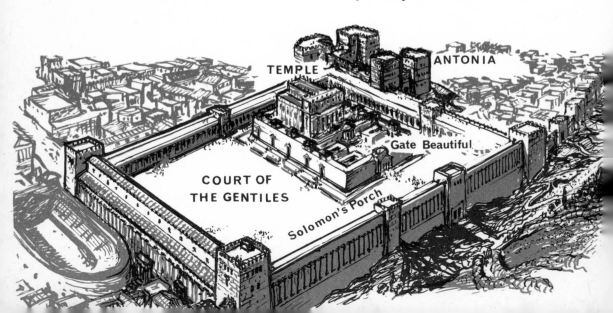

TEMPLE ANTONIA

Gate Beautiful

COURT OF
THE GENTILES

Solomon's Porch

To find and read in your bible

To draw

Draw a plan of the temple area at Jerusalem to show the various courts. Name each one on your plan.

To model

Make a model of the temple at Jerusalem and its surrounding courts, labelling each one. Reference books will help you in finding out details of the temple building.

To report

Imagine that you were a newspaper reporter in Jerusalem. Write a report for your readers on the riot in the temple court when Paul was arrested. Your report may include interviews with Claudius Lysias, Paul himself, and Luke who had watched the whole affair.

To imagine

Imagine that you were Paul's young nephew. Write or tell the story of how you found out about the plot against Paul and how you made it known. Use your imagination in adding details to the story—for example, as to how you found out about the plot.

To write

Imagine that you were one of the two centurions who were ordered to escort Paul from Jerusalem to Caesarea. Write a letter home to your family in Rome telling them about this undertaking.

To act

Act the scene between Paul and Felix, the Governor, with his wife Drusilla (Acts 24. 24-25). Luke tells us very little about it, so that you can imagine the interview and tell in your own words what they would discuss. Felix will be getting rather frightened by Paul's talk of judgement in the life to come, and his wife getting angry at Paul's talk of pure living.

To compare

Imagine a conversation between two Jews of this time, comparing the two Governors, Felix and Festus. You can either act this as a scene, or make up a "script" of the conversation.

To draw

There are a number of dramatic scenes related in this chapter. Draw or paint a series of pictures, as a strip cartoon, of those which you think to be most interesting.

To chart

Make your own chart of the family-tree of Herod the Great, to help you understand the rulers of Palestine in New Testament times.

To re-write

Choose one of the speeches of Paul, mentioned in this chapter, to re-write in your own words. You can find the references above.

For girls

Use reference books to find out more about the fashions of Roman ladies. Both the sisters, Drusilla and Berenice, dressed with great pomp. Draw the two sisters together, showing their dress and hair-style etc. Make up a conversation between them about Paul, whom they had both met and heard.

For boys

Use reference books to find out more about Roman soldiers, their ranks, equipment etc. Draw each of the men mentioned in this chapter—chiliarch, centurion, foot-soldier, spearman. Make up a conversation between Claudius Lysias and one of his centurions in which they discuss the prisoner Paul.

To act

Choose one of the dramatic scenes related in this chapter to act as a group.

The Church at Rome

The voyage from Caesarea to Myra

Paul was to travel to Rome with a group of other prisoners. They would have been condemned criminals, being sent to die in the amphitheatre at Rome. Paul, a Roman Citizen as well as a man of importance, was given special consideration. Two of his faithful friends were with him. One was Luke, the Greek doctor, who was thus able to tell the adventurous story of Paul's voyage at first hand. The other was Aristarchus, a Christian from Thessalonica, who had been one of those seized and dragged into the theatre during the riot at Ephesus. Neither of them had any right to be on board. They may have come as Paul's "slaves" so as to be able to remain with him.

Paul was in the charge of a kindly centurion named Julius. Luke says that he was one of the "Augustan band". This was a "royal" cohort since it was named after the emperor Augustus himself. This may have been a cohort, stationed in Judaea, that had been specially honoured. Or this may have been a popular name for a separate group of officers who were detached from regular service to undertake special duties. Such men travelled widely on all kinds of missions, including the escort of special prisoners. Julius was kind and courteous in his treatment of Paul. It may have been through his influence that Paul was well treated when they finally reached Rome. Julius himself would have looked forward to the

journey. Special officers were almost all Italians. He would enjoy
a few days of leave at home after completing his mission.

The party embarked at Caesarea. There was little chance of a
ship sailing direct to Rome. Judaea exported little, apart from
fish, so that there were no regular sailings to Rome. Besides, it
was now the end of summer. Sea travel was dangerous in the
Mediterranean Sea after September 14. Voyages on the open sea

146

ended on November 11. There was no time to waste, hoping for
a ship sailing direct to Italy. The centurion Julius, in charge of the
whole party, decided to take a small coastal ship sailing up to
the Roman province of Asia. He should be able to get a ship to
Italy from one of its ports. If not, he could take his prisoners by
land across Greece, following the great Egnatian Highway.

On the second day out the ship called at Sidon. This was the oldest city of the Phoenicians, but Tyre, its daughter city, had grown more prosperous. Sidon is often mentioned in Old Testament times. From Sidon came Jezebel, wife of King Ahab of Israel, who was only prevented from wiping out the worship of God by the great prophet Elijah. The craftsmen of Sidon had helped to build the temple at Jerusalem. Jesus himself had travelled near the borders of Tyre and Sidon during his ministry in Galilee and had helped a Phoenician woman (Mark 7. 24-30). Now there were Christians at Sidon, friends of Paul. The kindly centurion gave Paul freedom to visit them during the stay in Sidon harbour.

Leaving Sidon, the small ship hugged the coasts of Phoenicia, Syria and Cilicia on its way northwards. It came from Adramyttium, a port of Asia Minor near Troas, so that it was sailing home for the winter. Luke records with surprise that it sailed to the east of the island of Cyprus, for, on his voyage to Palestine, his ship had sailed to the west. But this was the regular course and it brought the ship to Myra in fifteen days, as some manuscripts add.

The voyage from Myra
Myra had a key position on the south-west tip of Asia Minor. This made it an important and busy port. It was used especially by long-distance shipping crossing the Mediterranean Sea. The ruins of its theatre, cut in the cliff, show the prosperity of Myra.

It remained a leading port for centuries. One of its later bishops, St. Nicholas, was to become the patron saint of sailors in the stormy waters of the eastern Mediterranean Sea.

Julius found a ship at Myra. It was in the regular Roman shipping line which sailed from Alexandria to Italy, and Myra was an important port of call on this leading trade-route. These ships carried grain to Rome from North Africa, especially from Egypt, the "granary of Rome". Alexandria had become the chief port of Roman Egypt, especially because of the corn trade. Already the huge population of Rome had come to expect free grain. An emperor kept his popularity by giving the people free "bread and circuses". Shortage of corn would lead to riots. It might even endanger the emperor's position. That was why grain ships from Alexandria sailed even in dangerous weather.

The new ship was quite a large one for Roman times. With the party of Julius on board, the passengers and crew totalled 276 persons. But even the largest ships were only 1,500 tons. There were no instruments, such as compasses, to steer ships in those days. Sailors used the sun by day and the stars by night for navigating. On a cloudy night they had nothing by which to fix their position. Even the largest ships were helpless in Mediterranean storms. Sensible sailors took care to avoid rough waters and the stormy season of the year.

ITALY

Rome
Three Taverns
Appii Forum
Puteoli

Rhegium

Syracuse

Malta

GREECE

Troas

Adramy-
thium

Athens

Cos

Cnidus

Crete
Phoenix
Cauda
Fair Havens

Rhod

MEDITERRANEAN

SYRTIS

NORTH AFRICA

miles

0   100   200   300

St. Paul's Bay

MALTA

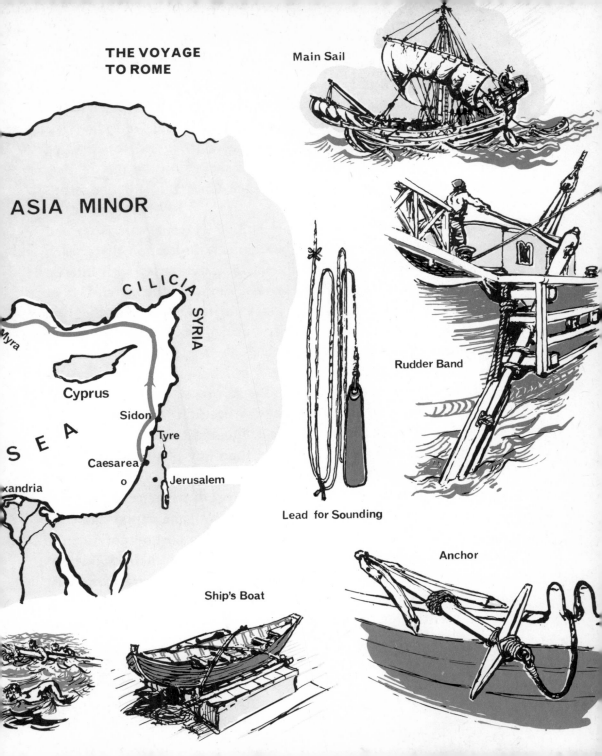

THE VOYAGE TO ROME

Main Sail

ASIA MINOR

CILICIA

SYRIA

Myra

Cyprus

Sidon

Tyre

S E A

Caesarea

xandria

o

Jerusalem

Rudder Band

Lead for Sounding

Anchor

Ship's Boat

The grain ship made first for the harbour of Cnidus, a city on the tip of Asia Minor, near the islands of Cos and Rhodes. But the winds delayed it and prevented it entering harbour. It therefore turned south towards the large island of Crete. Avoiding the dangerous north coast of the island, the ship passed round Cape Salome on the eastern coast. It found shelter on the Bay of Fair Havens on the south, protected by the land from the dangerous northerly winds.

The ship stayed for some time at Fair Havens, safe from bad weather. But there would not be complete protection there when the stormy winter season really set in. Luke notes with interest that, during their stay at Fair Havens, Paul kept the sacred Day of Atonement, with the customary solemn fast. It fell on the 10th day of the Jewish month of Tishri, our September-October. It was the climax of the ten days of penitence for sin with which the Jewish New Year began.

Time was now very short, with the stormy season close at hand. The centurion Julius had to make a decision. He discussed the situation with the captain and the sailing-master of the ship. Paul, who had more experience of travel than any of them, was asked for his views. He strongly advised staying at Fair Havens for the winter. To go on would endanger the lives of passengers and crew, as well as the safety of the cargo. But both the captain and the ship-master were for going on to the safer harbour of Phenice (Phoenix), about forty miles west, and wintering there. Julius was in charge. The Romans did not separate their army from their navy, and there was no doubt as to which was the more important. Julius was the senior officer present, and he was therefore respon-

SAILING SHIPS IN A STORM
This Roman relief, of the third century A.D. shows three sailing ships strug-
gling with a rough sea. On the left of the relief is a look-out tower. On the right
is one of the lighthouses which the Romans built along the coasts of the
Mediterranean with their usual thoroughness.

sible. He decided to follow the advice of the professional sailors.
The ship would go on to Phoenix for the winter.

The shipwreck

A pleasant south wind gave the opportunity to sail on from Fair
Havens, and to round Cape Matapan on the way to Phoenix. But
the winter haven was never to be reached. A fierce "north-easter"
suddenly blew up. It came down from the mountains of Crete
and was known as the "Euraquilo", the violent gale that struck
suddenly in autumn and spring. Ships of ancient times, with only
one main-sail, could only run before such a gale. Paul's ship was
fortunately blown close to the little island of Cauda, off the south-
west of Crete. Here the crew strengthened the ship. They "under-
girded" it—that is, they passed stout ropes around it to keep the
planks together. Trussing the ship would save it from sinking, for
the grain would swell with the water and burst the planks apart.

153

Another great danger faced the ship. If it were left to run before the north-east gale it would be heading straight for Syrtis—the dreaded banks of quicksands off the coast of North Africa. They stretched for 300 miles and many a ship had been sucked into them. The only answer to this awful threat was to lower the mainsail almost completely, leaving just enough to give some control over the ship's direction. Now the crew strove to head her westwards although, in the tempest, they had nothing to steer by. To Luke, knowing little about sailing, the ship seemed to be driven helplessly up and down the sea.

The situation was desperate. The ship's tackle and furniture and

A merchant ship returns safely from a voyage
The ship is entering Ostia, the port of Rome, The captain offers a sacrifice to the gods, for a safe voyage, on the poop. The background shows the statues of Neptune and other gods on the harbour wall.

most of the cargo were thrown overboard to lighten the ship. It was now that Paul showed his leadership and his staunch faith, giving fresh heart to everyone on board. As in other crises of his life, he had a vision during the night. He told everyone of his dream. He himself was to appear before Caesar at Rome. The ship would be wrecked on an island, but no one on board would be lost.

For fourteen days and nights the ship was at the mercy of the storm. Then, at midnight, the sailors' intuition told them that land was near. The line showed twenty fathoms, then only fifteen. The crew had to drop four anchors to hold the ship and to keep it off any rocks near the coast. They were lowered from the stern so that the ship's prow would be facing land, and make it easier to run ashore. Now they had to wait for daylight. But some of the crew could only think of saving their own skins. They began to lower the boat at the front of the ship, pretending that they were lowering more anchors. The observant Paul at once warned Julius. Without skilled seamen to man the ship, everyone on board would be in danger when they tried to beach it. The centurion at once ordered the ropes to be cut, letting the boat go free.

Again Paul showed his practical leadership. He advised everyone to eat, as they waited for daylight, so as to give themselves strength, after days without food, for the ordeal of getting ashore. He himself set an example, breaking bread and giving thanks to God before eating. Everyone followed him, heartened by his assurance that no one would be lost. The rest of the grain was thrown overboard so as to lighten the ship for driving ashore.

Daylight showed a creek. The anchors were raised and the ship aimed for it. But the front of the ship ran aground on mud, off a strip of land jutting out from the shore, while the stern was pounded and smashed by the seas. The soldiers were for killing the prisoners so that none of them could swim off and escape. Julius forbade them, wanting to save Paul. He ordered all who could swim to make for land first. The rest followed, some on planks and others on the backs of swimmers. Everyone on board came safely ashore, without loss, as Paul had foretold.

The island of Malta

The ship had been wrecked off the north-eastern shore of the island of Melita—known today as Malta. Still today the place of the shipwreck is known as St. Paul's Bay. Malta is the largest of three islands lying in a group between Sicily and North Africa. Malta itself is 62 miles from Sicily. All through history it has been an inhabited island. To the sailors of Phoenicia it was a strategic centre in the Mediterranean for their sea trade, and still today a Phoenician dialect is spoken on the island of Malta. Greeks had settled there, too, naming the island after the honey (Greek "meli") which it produced. Malta had become part of the Roman empire after Rome had conquered the Phoenician people of Carthage.

AN OBELISK FOUND ON THE ISLAND OF MALTA

This obelisk had been set up by two Phoenicians. It was dedicated to Mel-cart (Heracles), the god of Tyre. The dedication is written in two languages, Phoenician and Greek. It illustrates the mixed population on the island, using different languages.

156

Luke naturally calls the people of the island "barbarians"—the Greek term for all peoples who did not speak the Greek language or follow the Greek way of life. He certainly does not mean that they were savages, as our use of the word "barbarians" suggest. Indeed, he tells of the great kindness of the people of the island. The shipwreck had happened in mid-November. Warmth and food and shelter were needed in the cold and damp of winter. The islanders gladly provided them.

Paul made a great impression on the superstitious islanders. He had made a fire with sticks, when they came ashore, practical as he always was. A snake, slithering from the heat, wrapped itself around his arm. The islanders believed that it was poisonous, and they were astonished when Paul shook it off unharmed. They decided that Paul must be a god. They were still more impressed when Paul healed the sick. He healed the fevered father of Publius, the "chief man of the island", who had given hospitality to Paul and his companions. This title has been found on inscriptions, and it shows once again how accurate Luke was in writing his history. Other sick people were brought to Paul for healing. His party were loaded with gifts during the rest of their stay on the island.

The journey to Rome

After three months, the better weather of late February made sailing possible again. The party boarded the *Castor and Pollux*, another corn-ship from Alexandria, whose captain had wisely spent the whole winter at Malta. Castor and Pollux, twin gods of both Greeks and Romans, were believed to be friends of sailors. Seamen believed that they revealed themselves in "St. Elmo's Fire", the discharge of electricity from the atmosphere that sometimes hovers around the mast of a ship during storms.

A south wind was the signal for sailing. It carried the ship up to Syracuse but then it dropped, forcing the ship to linger there for three days. The city of Syracuse lies at the south-eastern corner of the island of Sicily. It had been founded by Greeks from Corinth in the eighth century B.C. Still today can be seen the remains of its Temple of Athena, the pride of Syracuse in Paul's time, as well as the amphitheatre, cut in the rock, that had been constructed with wonderfully exact measurements.

A slight change of wind meant that the ship had to tack across the Straits of Messina from Syracuse to Rhegium. This was another Greek city, known today as Reggio, on the toe of the mainland of Italy. Legend made it the home of Scylla, the dreaded sea-monster with twelve feet and six heads, which was believed to lurk in the Straits of Messina and to snatch sailors off the decks of their ships. Ships trying to avoid the dreaded Scylla might be sucked into the whirlpool of Charybdis, opposite Rhegium. Such terrifying superstitions made travelling by sea even more fearful than it really was.

THE ROMAN HARBOUR AT PUTEOLI
Based on a painting found at Pompeii.

After only one day at Rhegium, the south wind blew again. The *Castor and Pollux* had a smooth trip on to the port of Puteoli, today Pozzuoli, eight miles west of Naples. Fine roads led from Puteoli to Rome, 141 miles away. That was why grainships ended their voyage here, rather than sailing on to Ostia, the port of Rome. The huge amphitheatre at Puteoli was built a few years after Paul's arrival there. A painting found at Pompeii shows the harbour of Puteoli, busy with shipping, as Paul would have seen it. Such a large town already had a group of Christians, and Paul was permitted to stay with them for seven days.

From Puteoli the famous Appian Way, the "queen of Roman roads", led direct to Rome. It had been begun in 312 B.C. by a Roman official named Appius Claudius. It had been lengthened in later times till it ran the whole way from Rome to Brundisium, the modern Brindisi. There it linked by sea with the Via Egnatia across Greece, so that the Appian Way was part of the great Roman highway to the east. The road, laid on a well-prepared base of flint and stone, was 14 feet wide. The surface, made of stone blocks bound together with cement, was indestructible. The last 56 miles of the Appian Way were dead straight. Archaeologists have uncovered about 2 miles of it, as it approaches Rome. Thus it can be seen today as it was when Paul travelled along it, lined with tombs and monuments which, by Roman law, had to be outside city boundaries.

Byzantium

*The Appian way near Rome
in the time of St. Paul*

**THE APPIAN WAY—HIGHWAY
TO THE EAST**

miles

0   150   300

100 miles of travel along the Appian Way brought the party of prisoners to Appii Forum, the Market of Appius, forty miles from Rome. News of Paul's coming had already reached the Christians of the city, and he was greatly cheered when a group of them came to welcome him at this small hamlet. It was just the same at Three Taverns, 30 miles from Rome. Paul, who had had nothing to do with the church at Rome, was heartened to receive such a brotherly welcome. Thus he reached his goal, Rome itself, accompanied by the faithful Luke and Aristarchus and by Christians of the city.

Paul at Rome

The centurion Julius handed Paul over to his superior officer in the royal cohort of imperial couriers. Paul was allowed to live in his own hired house, as he awaited his trial. He was confined to it, with a soldier as constant guard, bound to him by a light chain. But he was free, as he had been at Caesarea, to receive any visitors, to hold meetings in his lodgings, to have his assistants with him and to keep in touch with his churches by messengers and letters.

Luke tells of an early meeting with the leaders of the Jewish synagogues at Rome. Paul would naturally desire to meet them and, in particular, to know what their attitude would be at his coming trial. They said that they had received no despatches from Judaea concerning Paul. They knew nothing about him, nor about his Christian teaching. They asked to come again to learn more about it. This time Paul spoke at length of how all the prophecies of the Jews had been fulfilled in Jesus. The result was as it had always been with Jews. Some believed, but many more were hostile. Once again Paul had to say that, since Jews rejected the promised Messiah, the Good News must be offered to Gentiles.

Luke concludes his history there, with this last record of Jewish hostility. He simply adds that Paul spent two years in his hired house, continuing his work for the Gospel. This was a triumphant climax to his history. Paul, its hero, had reached Rome itself, even if as a prisoner. The Good News of Jesus, first preached by a small group of Jews in faraway Jerusalem, had now spread throughout the Roman world and reached the very heart of the empire.

Paul and the church at Rome

Paul had played no part in founding the church at Rome. He had sent a letter to the Christians at Rome, some years before, telling them of his great hope to visit them. In it he had spoken glowingly of their church as being famed everywhere for its faith. But he had also written tactfully that he would not build on another man's foundations.

Paul may have been referring to the apostle Peter, who had certainly made one or more visits to Rome. We do not know how a church started at Rome, for the evidence is scanty and confusing. We saw how Paul had lived and worked at Corinth with the tent-makers, Aquila and Priscilla, Christian Jews who had been expelled from Rome. It was probably through such humble folk —craftsmen, traders, soldiers, slaves—that a church grew up at Rome. In one of his letters from prison, Paul sends greetings from Christians among Caesar's household (Philippians 4. 22). They would be slaves, but it was not long before Christianity spread to the upper ranks of Roman society. It seems that, in the beginning, the church at Rome was made up of Christians from abroad, rather than from converts in Rome itself. It used Greek as its language, rather than the Latin language of the Romans, for many years to come.

The end of Paul

Luke ended his history with Paul's confinement at Rome for two years, awaiting trial. He may not even have known of Paul's end when he wrote. Even if he had known, it would not have fitted in with his purpose to show how Paul had been put to death by Rome. His book, like his Gospel, was written for a Roman official. He was showing, all through his history, the hostility of the Jews and the friendliness of the Romans to the Christian preaching. To end with Paul's execution by the Romans would have contradicted the whole book. Or again, Luke may have intended to write a third book. He might have written such a book, now lost. We just cannot be sure.

Paul may have been tried, and executed at the end of his two years of confinement at Rome. But Clement, a bishop of Rome, in a letter written about 35 years late, implied that Paul had reached Spain. Other slight evidence suggests that Paul may have made another journey to the east, too. Thus, some think that Paul was tried and released after those two years, and went on further missionary journeys. Then, arrested once more, he was brought to Rome for a second time and put to death.

Strong tradition in the church said that both Peter and Paul died at Rome under the emperor Nero in A.D. 64. Nero had blamed Christians for the great fire of Rome, that summer, which rumour said had been started by Nero himself. In the persecution which followed, Peter and Paul were both imprisoned in the Mamertine prison, off the Roman forum. Paul died, tradition said, just outside the city on the Ostian Way which led to Ostia the port of Rome. It was the privilege of a Roman Citizen to die by beheading. Paul was executed at Salvian Springs, a pine wood beside the road.

Peter, said early tradition, was crucified in the Circus on Vatican Hill. This was a race-course that the emperor Caligula had made in his gardens for his own pleasure. Many Christians died here, during Nero's persecution, and were buried nearby. The first Basilica of St. Peter was built on this site. One of the many memorials found beneath it, in recent years, is thought to mark the place where Peter died, if not to have been his tomb.

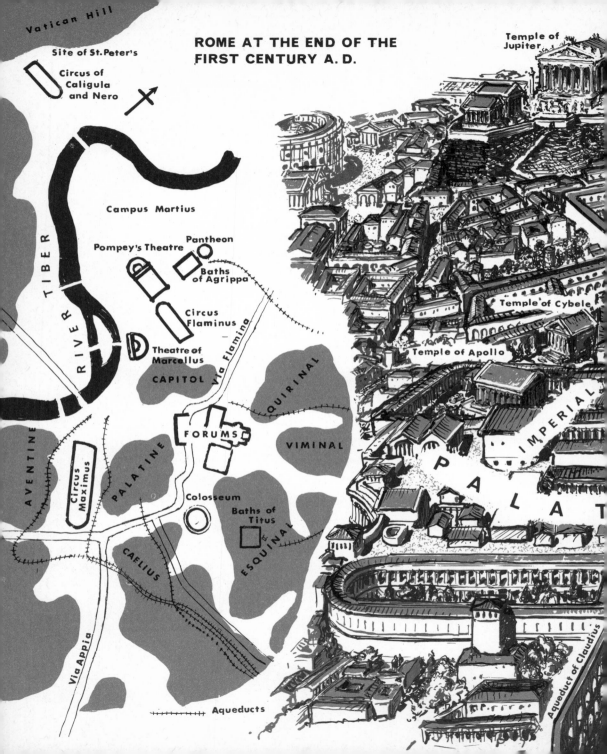

ROME AT THE END OF THE FIRST CENTURY A.D.

Vatican Hill

Site of St. Peter's

Circus of Caligula and Nero

Temple of Jupiter

Campus Martius

RIVER TIBER

Pompey's Theatre

Pantheon

Baths of Agrippa

Circus Flaminus

Theatre of Marcellus

Via Flamina

CAPITOL

QUIRINAL

VIMINAL

FORUMS

AVENTINE

Circus Maximus

PALATINE

Colosseum

Baths of Titus

ESQUINAL

CAELIUS

Via Appia

Aqueducts

Temple of Cybele

Temple of Apollo

IMPERIAL

PALAT

Aqueduct of Claudius

Thus the work of these two great apostles was done, and the church at Rome could for ever boast of them as being among its early leaders. Peter had come to Rome direct from Palestine. Paul had travelled through Crete, Asia Minor and Greece to reach his goal, planting the Church of Jesus among men of all nations. Now the great Apostle of the Gentiles was gone. But he had made sure that the Christian Church, built on sure foundations, would endure throughout the centuries to come, taking the Good News of Jesus to all mankind.

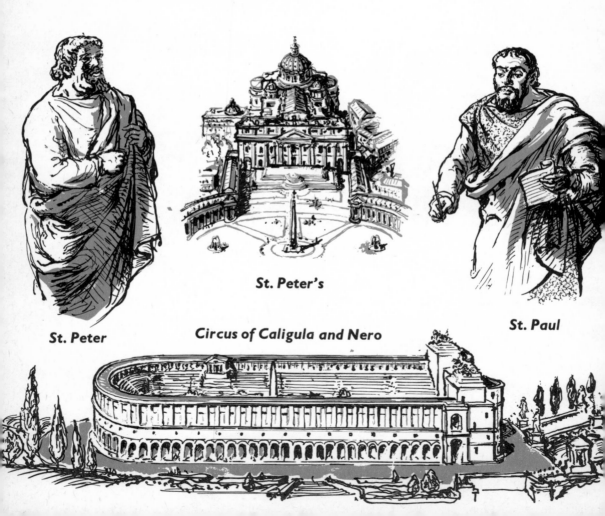

St. Peter's

St. Peter

Circus of Caligula and Nero

St. Paul

To find and read in your Bible

The voyage from Caesarea to Myra	Acts 27. 1-5
From Myra to Fair Havens	Acts 27. 6-12
Undergirding the ship at Cauda	Acts 27. 13-17
The north-easter called Euraquilo	Acts 27. 18-20
Paul's vision	Acts 27. 21-26
The shipwreck at Malta	Acts 27. 27-44
On the island of Malta	Acts 28. 1-10
The voyage to Puteoli	Acts 28. 11-14
On the Appian Way	Acts 28. 14-15
Paul at Rome	Acts 28. 16
Paul and the leaders of the synagogues	Acts 28. 17-29
Paul's confinement at Rome	Acts 28. 30-31

To map

Make your own map of the voyage of Paul from Caesarea to Italy, showing on it the places mentioned in this chapter.

To record

Imagine that you were Luke, the Greek doctor, who was with Paul throughout the journey from Caesarea to Rome. Make a diary of the voyage, to use later in writing your history book, with notes on all that happened.

To imagine

Imagine that you were Julius, the Roman centurion in charge of Paul. Write or tell the story of your adventures on the journey to Rome, as he would have told it to his family in Italy when he had competed his mission.

To draw

Draw a series of pictures, as a strip cartoon, of the journey from Caesarea to Rome, showing the main events.

To research

Use reference books to find out more about sea travel in Roman times. Write an account of what you find, with your own drawings. You may like to make this the story of a ship—say the *Castor and Pollux*—telling of its building, its equipment, its crew and how they sailed her.

To imagine

Imagine that you were one of the guards to whom Paul was chained during the two years in his hired house at Rome. Describe your impressions of Paul—his activities each day, his friends and visitors, the influence that he had on people through his faith and courage, and the effect that he had on you.

To act

Act the scene between Julius the centurion, the captain, the ship-master and Paul at Fair Havens. They are discussing what to do now that the stormy season is approaching, and each has his own reasons for going on or staying in the bay.

To plan

Plan a Service "For Those at Sea" which might be used in School Assembly. Find, in particular, a hymn tune named "Melita" and say how you think it got its name. The words to which it is sung will be very suitable for your Service. For a reading you might use Psalm 107. 23-31 or Jonah 2. 5-9, or, of course, part of the story of Paul's shipwreck. Make up your own prayers if you can.

To test your reading
See if you can explain the meaning of these words or phrases which you have read about in this chapter—Augustan cohort; "the granary of Rome"; "bread and circuses"; under-girding a ship; Syrtis; Melita; barbarians; St. Elmo's Fire; Scylla and Charybdis; Appian Way.

A play to write
Now that you have read the whole story of the life of Paul, join together in writing a script for tape-recording. You can do this as a play in separate scenes, choosing for your scenes the main episodes in Paul's life. Or you can write this as a television script, in the form of a documentary, including interviews with people who knew him. Each group can be responsible for a separate scene or part of the script. Use reference books as necessary.

A frieze to design
The whole class could join, too, in making a frieze of the life of Paul. It would show scenes from his life, as well as the background of his life, for display on the classroom wall.

A service to plan
Paul is remembered each year on January 25 in Christian churches. Plan a Service for his day, choosing hymns and readings which you think suitable. Compose your own prayers if you can.

Index

ROMANS	JEWS
EMPEROR AUGUSTUS (31 B.C.–A.D. 14) EMPEROR TIBERIUS (14–37)	HEROD THE GREAT (37–4 B.C.) ARCHELAUS HEROD ANTIPAS PHILIP PONTIUS PILATE—GOVERNOR (26–36) KING HEROD AGRIPPA I (37–44)
EMPEROR CALIGULA (37–41) EMPEROR CLAUDIUS (41–54)	
EMPEROR NERO (54–68)	HEROD AGRIPPA II (53–70) FELIX—GOVERNOR FESTUS—GOVERNOR
EMPEROR VESPASIAN (69–79) EMPEROR TITUS (79–81) EMPEROR DOMITIAN (81–96) EMPEROR TRAJAN (98–117)	JEWISH REVOLT: JERUSALEM AND TEMPLE DESTROYED (70)
	JEWISH REVOLT: 132 JEWS EXPELLED FROM JERUSALEM 135